D1078180

What to eat
when you can't eat anything
The Complete Allergy Cookbook

Chupi & Luke Sweetman

with a foreword by Patricia Quinn

and

photography by Suki Stuart

Newleaf

Dedication

Luke and I would like to dedicate this to Granny who couldn't boil an egg, and to Grandad who taught her how; to Michael and Patricia, our inspirational adopted grandparents; to Brian, our comrade in culinary crime; to Vanilla, the world's funkiest cat; and, of course, to our dearest 'Momager'.

Cheers!

Newleaf
an imprint of
Gill & Macmillan Ltd
Hume Avenue, Park West, Dublin 12
with associated companies throughout the world
www.gillmacmillan.ie

© Chupi and Luke Sweetman 2003
0 7171 3646 9
Index compiled by Cover to Cover
Design and print origination by Slick Fish Design
Printed by GraphyCems Ltd, Spain

This book is typeset in 8.5 point Caecilia on 13 point leading.

The paper used in this book is made from the wood pulp of managed forests. For every tree felled, at least one tree is planted, thereby renewing natural resources.

A CIP catalogue record is available for this book from the British Library.

Contents

Thank you's

To Patricia and Michael Quinn, the world's greatest nutritionist and enthusiast respectively. Thank you so so much.

To Mary, Philip and Peter, our darling friendies. To Kali, Jay and Siobhan, glad you like the pizza! To Libby and Naoise, dedicated tasters. To Emma, Matt, Brigid, Holly and Hazel, we love you guys! To Ruadhri, the adventurous vegetarian. To Eithne, for all the wonderful reviews she is going to give us. To Anna, Catherine and Libby, for the props. To Barry, fervent thanks for the moral support. To Doña Theresa, Muchas Gracias. To Francie, the kitchen counter king. To Ger Nichol, the queen of literary agents. To Will the Postie, cheers for the fantastic veggies. To Deirdre McQuillan, thank you, thank you, thank you! To the Durneys, for all the garlic and publishing advice. To Yardy, Muttly and Felix, our underfed dustbins. And to Brian, webmaster extraordinaire: check out www.whattoeat.net.

To our publishers: Eveleen Coyle, who saw promise in our scribbles. To D Rennison Kunz, for guiding our darling book through the final stages. To Michael Gill for his enthusiasm (and for giving us our photos!). To Nicki Howard and Anita Ruane for our cover – although Luke thinks there should be more of him!

Chupi and Luke Sweetman
www.whattoeat.net

Foreword

On a lovely day in May, the Sweetman family of Chupi, Luke and Rosita came into my life. Chupi had come with her Mum for nutritional counselling and kinesiology. Chupi's history, given by Rosita and herself, included years of unexplained ill health. From questions answered by both Rosita and Chupi, it became very clear that a lot of the functions of our bodies which we healthy types take for granted were not happening for Chupi. Because her food was not being absorbed, her natural defence mechanisms were deprived of minerals and vitamins vital for healthy immunity, and the fats essential for healthy physical, mental and emotional development. Years of chronic ill health and stress, plus a water supply which was not suitable for drinking or even cooking, had taken a huge toll on Chupi's health. In spite of all this, I found Chupi to be a happy, contented teenager with lots of enthusiasm for living and great ambition.

As is increasingly common among the people who attend my clinic, Chupi's digestion turned out to be a big part of the problem. It was failing to absorb her food and her intestinal immunity was poor, due to a proliferation of yeasts and unfriendly bacteria. The domino effect was poor resistance to infection, poor quality blood, poor healing ability and multiple food intolerances. The priority was to put my tried and tested structure in place, to encourage Chupi's body to heal itself:

1. A menu full of good, natural, tasty wholefood.
2. Perfectly clear water to drink, cook and bathe in.
3. Getting all the defence mechanisms back to work with good food, good water, rest, exercise and sunshine.
4. Chupi would need to rest for a few minutes before, and again after, each meal.
5. She would take an Acidophilus supplement to boost her natural defence mechanisms, boost her digestive ability and help her to fully absorb her good food.
6. Changing her menu included switching to completely unprocessed food: yeast free, dairy free, wheat free and sugar free, additive, colour and preservative free.

As with all my patients, it was a real challenge for the family. When they went home there was literally nothing they could eat. Two starving teenagers and a very depleted Mum. What a shock! But they fully took on what I had prescribed and gradually they learned how to cope as a family.

During Chupi's next visit, a wonderful summer day, it became obvious that she was on the road to recovery. She was extremely hungry, an excellent sign of life, because her body was like a plant adapting to new food. Her mum, herself and Luke were all involved in cooking wonderful foods – and they were loving them. We arranged a meeting where we could discuss this new adventure in food, cooking and creativity.

We agreed to share their new cooking creations with the recipes our family had been collecting for years, many of them adapted from our own mothers' healthy dishes. To make them even more healthy, we had moved away from commercial wheat, cut out refined sugar, yeasts and moulds, and introduced a wide range of flours, beans, seeds, nuts and vegetables, all organically produced where possible. As a family, we had been practising what we preached for the past thirty years. This had proved to be the biggest step towards good health. We did not cut out meat, we just reduced it in favour of lots more vegetables, brown rice and pastas. When we do eat meat, we try to eat only organically-produced, additive-free products.

The road to good health rests in the quality, quantity, preparation, cooking and, very importantly, the serving of beautiful, unadulterated food. It is life-giving, blood-building, bone-creating, brain-nurturing, mood-healing, emotionally-satisfying and tastes wonderful. This is what Rosita, Chupi and Luke were discovering. They found that their craving for unnatural, unwholesome foods faded away gradually, because wholefoods are so satisfying.

Following our discussions, we decided to have a 'tasting' day and share our cooking experiences. My husband Michael and I drove to the Sweetman home, the boot of our car laden with chickpea and chicken casserole with herbs in organic tomato sauce, muffins made of wholemeal flour, fruit and a bottle of Amé to celebrate! When we brought our contribution to the kitchen, Luke was cooking a wonderful steak with tons of vegetables, Rosita had a made beautiful vegetable soup with homemade stock and Chupi had made spelt farls and spelt biscuits (Italian, twice-baked biscuits). Chupi and Luke had also made delicious date and orange squares, which emitted an aroma of warm welcome and a warmer taste sensation.

As we exchanged recipes, a thought planted itself: we should gather all the work of both houses together. Everyone was benefiting, our conversations were exhilarating, we were seeing the family's health change. Why not collaborate? We decided to gather up our learning and our recipes, and put them together into an allergy cookbook for all those who found themselves in the same position as Rosita, Chupi and Luke. The book would be for allergy sufferers, for the very sensitive, the not-so-sensitive, and for those who want to eat beautiful food – perfectly well people who wish to remain in good health. This idea coincided with Chupi and Luke studying for their Junior and Leaving Certificates – at home. A busy time all round!

The change of every season is an acknowledged strain on the body, and all the more so for the very young, the teens and the elderly – the sensitive. Our family meetings to discuss food and health became ideal opportunities to monitor Chupi's health through the seasons of the year. Each season's change meant a change for her: seasonal food, local produce, careful pacing of her energy. If the change of the season is from spring to a glorious May or June, this is a plus factor. Our Irish summers and springs seem to be wetter, damper and less sunny than before, so as often happens at the end of summer and autumn, overnight we can find ourselves in new weather. This is where we need to balance with the environment. Because young people tend to work hard and play hard, this is a difficult lesson to learn – but it pays great dividends in protection from winter chills.

After having been part of an allergic family myself, and taking care of severely allergic families for thirty years, it is clear to me that it is always necessary to find a replacement food for the one removed, however temporarily. Most people are sensitive to foods they (probably) eat far too regularly. Traditional eating with the seasons in past times was a form of protection against developing sensitivities, but today we are encouraged to eat our favourite foods all year round. Real allergic reactions are infrequent, but they are increasing due to the drastic changes in our eating habits and the ways in which our food is produced using chemicals and pesticides.

Both Chupi and Luke achieved tremendous success in their studies and exams. Chupi decided to take a year off instead of going to college, in order to write this cookery book. With great zest and creativity the recipes were tried, tested and committed to paper. As we now read through the manuscript just after Christmas 2002, we are excited: the aromas jump off the pages with the wonderful combinations of foods, herbs, spices. Good health begins with your choice of food. It manifests itself in the dishes prepared in your kitchen as it nourishes the body today and creates the health of tomorrow.

Daily, in my practice, people ask me what to eat and where they can find a book that shows them what to eat: after thirty years of searching, this is that book.

Patricia Quinn

The Story of Food

In this affluent wedge of the planet, food is not the problem. Here in the West we are surrounded by (literally) mountains of food. Food is everywhere – in supermarkets, restaurants, corner shops, cinemas, shopping centres, fast-food outlets, even garages. The problem, however, is what to eat of the food that abounds, how to discriminate so that our food supports and nourishes us as often as possible, makes us smack our lips and yell, 'Wow! That was delicious.' The irony is that the more food there is in our Western world, the more food-related illnesses appear, everything from allergies to obesity to cancer.

Our journey into what to eat began in the spring of 2000. Chupi was lying on the sofa and I was listening to an afternoon radio programme on different alternative medicine practices: homoeopathy, aromatherapy, *et al*. It was a very simple series, with a short introduction by the presenter, followed by an interview with the chosen practitioner. This week's turn was nutrition. To be honest, nutrition had never been a subject of passionate interest to me, but within minutes of listening to Patricia Quinn's clear-as-a-bell voice, I was riveted.

At the time, Chupi (then sixteen), Luke (then thirteen) and I were in health-hell. Chupi was just barely coping with daily living. Everyone we consulted gave us a different outcome, a different remedy, a different diagnosis. Chupi recoiled from them all, and I, being the Mum, was borderline insane with anxiety.

Now here was Patricia Quinn, a clear small voice in the babbling wilderness. She talked about the process of illness: fatigue which doesn't respond to rest; growing irritability; symptoms; and finally, illness. Her 'doctors' were sunlight and fresh air, pure water and good food, proper exercise and sufficient rest. Neither illness nor health are random nor inexplicable: they occur because of what has happened to us (or what we have done to ourselves). We can (and should) be actively involved in our own healing, following very simple guidelines, starting with rigorously sorting out our nutrition. As Darina Allen once famously remarked, none of us would dream of putting dodgy fuel into our precious cars, yet we routinely put the dodgiest of fuel into our bodies. We really are what we eat.

When Patricia saw Chupi for the first time, she diagnosed, along with other problems, an extremely severe Candida Albicans infestation. Candida Albicans, a yeast common to our digestive systems, usually becomes a problem – sometimes a life-threatening one – when a combination of factors trigger an explosion/overgrowth. The most common trigger is overuse of antibiotics (these wipe out the friendly bacteria in the gut and the ever opportunistic Candida takes hold), and then too much sugar, yeast and refined, processed wheat in the diet, along with prolonged stress. Candida keeps its hold and gets ever stronger as a weakened immune/digestive system is unable to reassert control by normal methods. The only cure is to go off all sugar and yeast and any foods that have any traces of yeast or mould. No biscuits, no cakes, no shop-bought pizzas, no fast foods, no alcohol, no vinegar, no shop-bought condiments are allowed. As Patricia explained, the only way to control Candida is to stop feeding it. (There is no conventional cure for Candida, in fact conventional medicine's overuse of antibiotics is centrally implicated in the huge rise of Candida in the West. Candida sufferers are forced to take a natural path to healing.) Our task was twofold: to get Chupi off all Candida-feeding foods, and to build her health back up by putting her on a good, clean, healthy diet.

The first few weeks of the diet were pandemonium. Chupi was permanently starving. Luke and I were permanently cooking. No yeast and no sugar meant no supermarket-bought food and no processed or pre-cooked food, since virtually all such food is bulked up with wheat, yeast, sugars and additives such as monosodium glutamate (MSG). For those of you who pride yourselves on living clean, just think MSG, the most common flavour-enhancing substance around, is apparently the second most addictive substance on the planet, crack cocaine being the first.

Gradually, as Chupi's system got stronger and Luke and I got better in the kitchen, our diet (and stamina) improved. We found friends who ordered wholefood and would put in an extra order for us. The same friends told us of a local organic farm where you can buy boxes of organic, seasonal vegetables every week. A health food shop opened locally. We discovered the Temple Bar Organic Food Market in Dublin and went there every Saturday without fail.

One of the biggest problems we encountered was finding recipes that didn't involve soaking obscure beans for 100 years, cooking them for 500 years, then covering the resultant goo with concentrated apple juice. Chupi and Luke were teenagers, they needed nutritious and tasty food – obscure beans just weren't going to do the trick. We had to stick to the diet, and if we were going to succeed, we had to make it delicious. *What to eat* was born, like many good ideas, points out Patricia, at the kitchen table. Chupi was armed with notebook and pen, with Luke and I calling out – turmeric, 1 teaspoon! 2 cloves garlic, crushed! 1 can organic tomatoes! – as we assembled an evening's concoction.

This is an incredibly exciting time to be interested in food. With the agricultural system in turmoil – foot and mouth, mad cow disease, CJD, salmonella, e-coli and now GM – more and more people are turning towards organic food, grown locally, in season and without chemicals, pesticides or genetic meddling. In a 2002 article in *The Sunday Times* the professor of bacteriology who led the inquiry into the e-coli outbreak in England in 1996, in which twenty-one people were killed and 500 made ill, said e-coli is now endemic in 50 per cent of Britain's livestock herd and we 'ignore it at our peril'. With one in three people in Ireland now expected to develop cancer, more and more of us are wondering if the lethal cocktail of chemicals we have unleashed on nature is doing more harm than good. If chemicals and pesticides kill weevils, greenfly, and all those other

creepy crawlies that make life difficult for the food producer, then surely they're going to harm us too?

The food may look great on the supermarket shelves, but those glossy bright red apple skins have been produced by chemicals, not by nature. The build-up of toxins in our bloodstream, kidneys and livers will inexorably produce illness. In the globalisation of food production and marketing, real food has never been so compromised – genetically modified, drenched in pesticides, stored for far too long. More and more health practitioners see the over-production of yeast and mould in our systems – as a result of our sugar- and yeast-dependent diet – as the simmering cauldron from which a raft of modern-day illnesses, from thrush to ME, MS, asthma and cancer, develop. Cooking real, organic, natural, additive-free food has never been more important – for everyone in the family. *What to eat* believes that eating Green, eating organic, is no longer a lifestyle choice, but an absolute necessity.

But, an end to doom and gloom! Here are our recipes for good – and lasting, we hope – health. Where possible, the ingredients are organic; they are also sugar free, MSG free, wheat free (we use spelt flour in all the recipes), yeast and mould free, and of course GM free. They are for anyone suffering from Candida or food intolerances, but they're also – we hope you'll agree – delicious, and really good for everyone in the family, from baby to Granny.

This is our story, the story of the *What to eat when you can't eat anything* cookbook. Our hope is that all of you, whether suffering from health problems or not, will enjoy every single recipe in our book. As you get more and more into the story of cooking and food, you'll find food time becomes 'real time' where all of the household, family or friends, are involved. Meals will become what they truly should be: wonderful thanksgiving feasts, scrumptious and bursting with health, offering all the fruits of Mother Nature.

Enjoy!

Rosita Sweetman

The Green Diet

When we refer to a food as Green, this doesn't mean that it is or should be mouldy! Green is what we call our diet and the foods we find acceptable. None of our ingredients will harm you if you are sensitive. You may, however, have a particular problem; if so, you need to know as much about food as possible, so read on.

Diet affects everyone. Young and old, healthy and not so healthy, we are shaped and controlled by what we eat. If there is no energy in our food, should we be surprised when we have no energy? And if we eat food that is so processed it's poisonous, should we be surprised when our bodies show symptoms of poisoning?

When we sensitive types examine our diet, we need to consider the differences between allergies and intolerances. An allergy is systemic; it involves the whole body rejecting and mobilising to fight a foodstuff, sometimes with very dangerous results, e.g. anaphylactic shock. But a lot of what appear to be food allergies are in fact food intolerances. A food intolerance produces similar symptoms to a food allergy, but the reaction is not as violent because it is not systemic. We are born with an allergy as part of our system. Intolerances are developed for various reasons, such as stress. When the body is stressed, it becomes unable to cope with the most toxic foods.

The reactions in both intolerances and allergies may appear to be very similar, which is why it's hard to tell the difference, but with practice, experience, a little time and energy we can learn the difference. It is important to be able to tell the difference because, in general, intolerances can in greater part be overcome, but allergies need to be carefully managed.

This section of the book is specifically designed for those of you who would like more information on diets. We list the six main causes of allergies and intolerances: wheat, sugar, yeast, dairy products, gluten, and artificial additives, with a description of each food, symptoms of reactions to each food, why you could be intolerant, how to remove the food from your diet and what to replace it with. We also give what we hope is some useful information regarding organic foods. In addition, there is a guide on when our recipes should be eaten. The recipes are in three categories: ultra-sensitive, sensitive and un-sensitive. This section should help in your search for a better understanding of food and its relationship with your body. When Chupi was diagnosed we remember how confusing and depressing were the allergy books we read, and the fact that her new diet was meant to centre around beans. So we have tried to make these recipes as intelligible and interesting as possible.

Wheat

Grain is a wonderful substance, nourishing and health-giving, but by the time most grains reach us they are nothing more than a worthless plumper. Wheat, often labelled as starch or modified starch, is a perfect example of this. When commercially produced wheat arrives at your table, it will have been covered in pesticides and herbicides, grown on depleted soil with the aid of artificial fertilisers, and the nutritious germ and bran will have been removed. All we are left with is a 'powder' that will swiftly become glue when eaten. Even those with the most iron-clad digestion will have some problem digesting commercial wheat, and to those who are sensitive it's a nightmare. (Some people are not wheat intolerant, but are intolerant to the junk used on commercial wheat, so bear this in mind.)

Symptoms of intolerance A powdery feeling in the mouth, especially in the morning, Irritable Bowel Syndrome (IBS), bloating, painful digestion, constipation, diarrhoea, acid stomach, weight gain (or severe weight loss in

coeliac disease).

Replacement Wheat is in all – unless specifically labelled wheat-free – baking, breads, buns etc., pasta, flours, nearly all processed food, instant meals and take-aways as a bulking agent. If in doubt, read the label. We recommend you remove all 'normal' wheat from your diet. Replacing it depends on how intolerant you are; if you have only mild problems with wheat or feel you could do with a boost, then replace it with organic wheat and organic wheat products, using these as normal. If you are sensitive to wheat, replace it with organic spelt flour (available in health food shops). This flour is very similar to wheat, but tastier, and perfect for people with a wheat intolerance. You can use organic spelt products as you would wheat products. If you are highly wheat intolerant, or coeliac, then you will need to be very careful. Use rice, maize (corn) and gram flours, millet grain and a small amount of organic oats. Stay on this diet for four weeks then slowly introduce organic spelt flour; if your symptoms return, go back to the exclusion diet until you feel you're ready to try again. It is hard to say how long this can take: some people need only a few weeks, others longer. But in general we have found that 99 per cent of people can tolerate, and enjoy, organic spelt.

Sugar

Sugar – the villain of the piece. A highly processed 'food', of no nutritional value, sugar confuses the body by providing false highs followed by compensatory lows. It encourages yeast overgrowth and is highly addictive. Few people know they are sugar intolerant, yet everyone could do with excluding it from their diet. This is not as easy as it may seem, however, as there are many sources of hidden sugar. Manufacturers realise this, and replace sugar content with artificial sweeteners which are equally bad (see Artificial Additives). In Eric Shlosser's book, *Fast Food Nation*, he estimates that the average American consumes 52 teaspoons of sugar per day, most of it hidden.

Symptoms of intolerance Mood swings, Candida and other yeast-related problems (e.g. acne, hypoglycaemia, skin problems, general itchiness).

Replacement Sugar is found in nearly all processed foods, sweets and treats, and take-aways, etc. unless they are specifically labelled sugar-free. Most sugar-free items, however, contain unpleasant sweeteners. Ask for advice from your local health food shop on alternatives to sugar-sweetened soft drinks and other products. Read the section called Yummy Treats for sweetie help too. If a recipe requires sugar, first consider if it really needs sweetening and, if it does, use local honey, rice syrup or maple syrup. When you give up sugar, honey will be your saviour. Sugar is also widely used in processed, pre-packed, ready-made and take-away meals: I'd recommend you eat none of these unless you are absolutely sure they are sugar-free and even then ...

Yeast

Yeasts and moulds are living organisms that thrive in warm, damp conditions, growing at enormous rates. When you eat a slice of bread, in that bread there are thousands of live yeast organisms passing through your stomach, and arriving in your warm, hospitable gut. The yeasts settle in and start to grow. If you are in full health your body's immune system will counteract them. But if your immune system is weak or you have just received a course of antibiotics, then the yeast will continue to grow. One particular yeast, Candida Albicans, can turn into a parasite (an organism that lives off another organism – in this case you) breaking through the delicate intestinal lining and allowing undigested food to leak into the bloodstream. Many people are allergic to yeast without knowing it. Patricia and Michael Quinn have written a book called *The Silent Disease* about Candida/yeast overgrowth. In the West we eat a diet and live a life conducive to yeast overgrowth: we eat a lot of sugar, which feeds the yeast. We consume a lot of other yeasts, for example in alcohol, follow a poor, junk-filled, diet and live our lives constantly stressed, allowing our immune systems to remain below par. Yeast overgrowth is also a major factor in intolerances – in fact in some cases it is the cause. If you remove all yeasts from your diet, you will see huge improvements.

Symptoms of intolerance Candida and related problems, acne, eczema, dandruff, psoriasis, fungal infections, irritable bowel syndrome, diarrhoea, constipation, thrush, allergies.

Replacement Unfortunately yeasts are found in all breads (except soda bread), alcohol, mushrooms, vinegars, soy sauces and tofu. You may be panicking at the thought of excluding all these products from your diet, but they can be replaced. For the breads use soda bread – if you can eat wheat and dairy products there are a few nice shop-bought ones; if not, make you own using our recipe (page 143). Sourdough breads are delicious, as long as you buy good ones. There is no alcohol replacement, you just have to give it all (yes, all) up. If you are absolutely desperate you can try very pure alcohol such as vodka – low in yeast. This won't work for everybody, however, and I wouldn't recommend it. Some people can eat mushrooms, others cannot. They should be avoided for the first few weeks at least. Vinegar can be replaced with freshly squeezed lemon juice. For soy sauce, just leave it out, it's only a trendy flavour enhancer. You can try it again when you feel up to it. Tofu is best avoided during the initial stages of your new diet, but it can be re-introduced later.

Dairy Produce

This means all milk and milk products, but for our book we have primarily excluded cow's milk, as most people who are intolerant to cow's milk can take goat's and sheep's milk produce. We don't use much dairy in our recipes anyway, so don't worry if you can't have it. Dairy intolerance is one of the most prevalent and the only answer is to reduce the amount of dairy you eat. Carefully managed and used sparingly, such products can be a tasty addition to our diets.

Symptoms of intolerance Acne, eczema, coated tongue, diarrhoea, blocked or runny nose, sinusitis, catarrh, Candida, thrush.

Replacement Milk, cream, milk solids, half-fat solids and whey are all dairy. Dairy clearly means all butter, cheese, milk, yoghurt, creams and ice-creams. It also tends to be in processed foods, such as ready-made soups. There are two paths to change: you can remove all dairy produce from your diet, especially if you are dairy intolerant, and replace with our list below; or you can remove all non-organic and hidden dairy products, but use very small amounts of organic dairy. We now follow the second path, having tried the first for a year. You will see that a few of our recipes use organic bio-live natural yoghurt, which I could eat even when I was intolerant as it's wonderfully soothing and packed with good bacteria, a great help if you're yeast-intolerant. Replace butter with a good extra-virgin olive oil or organic butter; cheese can be replaced with organic goat's or sheep's cheese. Many people can tolerate goat's or sheep's produce, even if they can't have cow's milk cheese. Replace cow's milk with oat, soya, rice or goat's milk. Yoghurt can be replaced with organic bio-live natural yoghurt, which also works as a cream substitute. If you can't have that, try a soya cream. Be careful, as some brands have lots of other harmful ingredients in them. Instead of ice-cream, use soya ice-cream or discover the joy of sorbet. Try Mango Sorbet (page 131).

Artificial Additives

So much of the food we now eat contains additives – a packet of crisps that doesn't contain E621 is a rarity. And yet as consumers, we know very little about these additives. Take E621, also known as monosodium glutamate (MSG). Used as a flavour enhancer in crisps and nearly every pre-packed food, MSG is a boon to food companies: add a dollop and everyone, young and old, will want to eat your product. Yet MSG is dangerous to babies and children, bad for asthma and hyperactivity and is highly addictive. Why would MSG affect you if you have a specific allergy? Well, if you have an allergy then your body is not at its full strength, so it is very important to be careful that everything you eat will strengthen your body as well as stimulate your taste buds. This also applies to artificial sweeteners. Many people, for example diabetics, give up sugar, rightly believing it to be bad for them. They then replace sugar with sweeteners, but artificial sweeteners are as bad as sugar – they are an empty food. One of the first mistakes I made when I gave up sugar was to eat a packet of sugar-free sweets that contained lots of artificial sweeteners. The effects were as bad, if not worse, than my reaction to normal sugar. So remember, if you don't know what it is, don't eat it.

Symptoms of intolerance Sudden onset of heartburn, skin reactions, itchiness, dizziness, stomach upset, mouth ulcers, asthma attack.

Replacement First identify what products you buy that contain potentially 'dodgy' ingredients. This will include nearly all processed, packaged, ready-made meals and all sweets and treats. Eliminate them from your diet. However, good crisps can be a saviour when you give up everything else, so find a brand you can eat, buy one packet and one apple and enjoy. In general, the plainer the crisps the better (e.g. just salt). Try the supermarkets, as there you get a wide selection and can also find the best. Tortilla crisps are worth checking out, as there are some very tasty flavours (I had chilli and cocoa!) that don't contain any junk. This advice applies to all foods that contain artificial additives – 90 per cent of the time you will be able to find a food to replace the junk one, the other 10 per cent was probably extremely bad for you and best not eaten anyway.

Gluten

Before reading this section, we strongly recommend that you read our wheat section first. The two reactions are so similar that it would be most unfortunate to mistake a gluten allergy/intolerance for the far less complicated wheat allergy/intolerance. Allergic reactions to gluten are becoming more common, and coeliac is another name for the true allergic reaction to gluten. Gluten is the 'gluey' protein contained in the starchy part of some grains. You can see it at work when you make porridge with oats – the way it sticks together and becomes glue-like is the gluten. If you are allergic to gluten, when you eat any grain containing it, your body will go through the normal digestive process until the gluten reaches the small intestine. Our small intestine is like a long pipe, the inside of which is lined with little digestive 'feelers' called villi; these absorb the nutrients from our food. However, if you are allergic to gluten, when it comes into contact with the villi, they swell up and your body simply cannot absorb any nutrients. You also experience a range of unpleasant symptoms.

Symptoms of intolerance Acid stomach, coated tongue, severe weight gain or loss, bloating.

Replacement Gluten is in many grains. All wheat products, including cous-cous, rye and oats have a low gluten content, so should be avoided by the true coeliac. Barley also has a low gluten content. Spelt flour also contains gluten, but seems to be tolerated by some – and I stress 'some' – people. Considering this, you're going to have to work hard to not eat gluten. No pre-packed/ready-made/bought foods are permitted unless they are from a wholefood supplier who understands the whole issue. You can eat buckwheat, chickpea/gram, cornmeal/maize, millet and rice products, as they are all gluten-free.

The three main areas where a gluten allergy/intolerance will affect your life are, first, bread; I can't enthuse about gluten-free bread, because it isn't great, but persevere and you'll get through. We do have a good gluten-free Tortilla, and a gluten-free bread. Then there's pasta: the two best we've found are rice-and-millet, and buckwheat; the others just seem to dissolve into a goo. Be careful when cooking gluten-free pasta, as it takes much less time to cook than ordinary pasta. Finally, there are sweets and treats; we have lots of yummy gluten-free treats, so hopefully they will help.

Try an exclusion diet for three weeks before you commit yourself to a gluten-free life. And, remember, it is possible to overcome a gluten problem. Good luck!

Organic

Organic farming is a return to traditional farming; no artificial fertilisers, pesticides or chemicals are used, plants are grown naturally and animals are reared with respect. And, with the US government trying to force its vast range of GM (genetically modified) foods into the European market, going organic has never been so important.

Sourcing organic products Try to locate an organic farm in your area and see if they run a box scheme (most do): this will be a box of organic, seasonal vegetables. If you try these, you will notice a difference in taste. Because organic food is far more labour intensive, it costs more, so switching completely to organic may not be feasible all in one go. Just change the really important foods such as **meat**. All meat you eat should be organic – there is no need to detail the endless list of problems with 'normal' meat (think BSE). You should not expose yourself, or the animals, to these risks. Organic meat can be found in most supermarkets, your local butcher or farmers' market; if you can't find any, then just ask.

The second most important area in which to go organic is **dairy** produce. If you're dairy intolerant, then this is irrelevant, but some people who are dairy intolerant can tolerate organic dairy. Try supermarkets for organic dairy – surprisingly enough they tend to be the best source of organic yoghurt, butter, cheese and milk.

As for **fruit and vegetables**, eat seasonally as much as possible, because food in season tends to be less chemical-laden. As I said above, there will also probably be an organic farm in your area that runs a box scheme. It's often cheaper than the supermarkets, you're supporting your local economy and you know exactly who is growing your food. The food actually looks and tastes organic, unlike the supermarket stuff! If all you can get is supermarket organic produce, it's better than nothing.

Then there are **grains and pulses**, store cupboard staples. Most are grown with extraordinary amounts of artificial chemicals, so do check out the organic alternative in your local health food shop. They will normally supply everything you need and will be happy to help.

The Right Recipes for the Right Time

As I've said before, we believe that when you're intolerant to foods it's not necessarily just a specific food that is a problem, but that your whole body is too stressed and thus unable to cope with certain very intense foods. This was certainly true in our case; we devised the Green diet, through accident, luck and pure hunger, to enable us to cope with eating. Yet the diet has been so successful that while at the start we needed to be very careful as we were ultra-sensitive, the good food has enabled us to progress to foods that we would never have been able to eat while ultra-sensitive. We then progressed to a sensitive stage, right up to now where we eat a good, practically un-sensitive diet. With this in mind we've divided the recipes into three categories: Ultra-Sensitive, Sensitive and Un-Sensitive. That's not to say the categories aren't interchangeable – these are simply a few guidelines to get you started. Listen to your body and always listen to what it's trying to say to you.

And, oh yeah, relax, you WILL get well.

Recipes for when you are ULTRA SENSITIVE

Ultra-sensitive is when you are intolerant to, or not eating, dairy, wheat, sugar, yeast, eggs and meat. You may be hypoglycaemic, with severe Candida, Chronic Fatigue, ME or Irritable Bowel Syndrome. Many people who are ultra-sensitive tend to be coeliac as well. With that in mind, we use all simple foods and cut out all junk (read the Different Diets section for more information on this).

Recipes for when you are SENSITIVE

When you are just sensitive, things are improving. Your intolerances will have calmed and you will be feeling better due to abstention from the causes of your problems. Your body will also be picking up, thanks to all the wonderful nutrition it has been getting. So now you can include some more foods in your diet, plus everything in the ultra-sensitive section.

You could try one of the pasta dishes now:

Recipes for when you are UN-SENSITIVE

You will now know what your allergies are and what your intolerances were, thus you can decide what is good for you and occasionally eat foods that are strong, e.g. organic dairy. You can eat everything under the previous two headings as well as everything below. Enjoy.

The Basics

These days people cook far less than they used to, which means that fewer people actually know how to cook. So here are the basics for the newly converted, and old hands, to cooking.

Cooking is both easy and enjoyable, not a chore to be dreaded. When we cook at home, we all cook – everyone, friends and family. Getting everyone involved when you cook makes it less work and more fun. The more people are involved in the cooking, the greater their interest in food. On this principle, put everyone on the same diet. Even if just one person in a house is sick, it really helps if everyone eats – at least some of the time – as the sensitive person does. Although many people feel they don't have the time to cook, a tasty pasta or soup can be whipped together in the time it takes to prepare convenience foods – and the difference in taste is incredible. Remember, food and cooking should be a joy, not a penance.

Always use the best ingredients, brand spankingly fresh and organic where possible. Organic is not simply about saving the planet, nor is it just about health. It is also about flavour: good ingredients make good food, and you can't get any better than organic.

In our recipes we recommend certain foods and ingredients, none of which should be too hard to find. Check out Food Resources if you're having problems (page 168).

Get to know your equipment. We cook on an ancient Aga and gas cooker, proof that there's no need for expensive kit. What you do need, however, is to know your equipment. Throughout the recipes we indicate, for example, 'a medium heat' or a 'low heat'; you will get to know how 'low' or 'high' suits your cooker and what its happy temperatures are. If you're in doubt, always err on the side of caution. For notes on equipment, see Tools of the Trade (page 170).

This is an allergy cookbook, but it is also a food cookbook. In the recipes, we use no sugar or yeast, as we feel they are too problematic. Occasionally we do use organic dairy, based on our personal experience that after an initial exclusion period, a small amount of organic dairy is acceptable and enhances the flavour. For flours we have given the option to use organic wheat, if you want to, in place of spelt flour, but we always use spelt as it's so good. In fact everything is up to you: if something isn't OK, replace it; if something is OK, use it.

Chupi Sweeman

Morning Foods

As we know only too well, morning is the most important time to eat, although it is also the most difficult time to eat. One of the things you will find when you switch to Green eating is that you'll be extremely hungry: eating in the morning is vital if you don't want to be gnawing the table leg by 10 a.m.! So our first recipe chapter is called Morning Foods to flag the importance of morning eating – the opposite of grabbing a styrofoam cappuccino and croissant en route to stressville.

In this chapter we hope to show that it is possible to make lots of delicious, hot, organic food in a short amount of time, just before you charge out to face the world.

Pinhead Porridge

Feeds 4: Porridge isn't very exciting and nor is it very tasty, if the only kind you've tried is the gooey mush made from normal oats. We've found that if you use pinhead oats the change in flavour is incredible. You get a sweet, chewy porridge, delicious with a milk of your choice (oat, rice, soya, goat's or cow's) and a big dollop of honey. The only downside is you have to soak the oats the night before, but then they do only take a few minutes to cook in the morning.

What you need: 2 cups **pinhead oat flakes**
6 cups/1.5 l **water**
milk (oat, rice, soya, goat's *or* organic cow's)
honey

What you do: Put the oats in a saucepan. Cover with 4 cm/2 in water. Leave to soak overnight. In the morning, put the saucepan on a medium heat, with another cup of water, and cook for 15–18 minutes, stirring occasionally. The oats are cooked when they've lost their crunch. Serve with milk and some honey.

Muesli

Makes 1 quantity: Muesli, with its mixture of oats, fruits and nuts, is one of the best ways to start the day. Once you start making your own, you'll never want to look at one of those shop-bought, sugar-laden travesties again. And, of course, be creative – add more of what you like and less of what you don't, using our recipe as a template. Another good idea is to make double or treble quantities and store in an airtight jar for during the week when you need an instant boost.

What you need: 2 cups **oat flakes**
2 cups **jumbo oat flakes**
1 cup **rye flakes**
1 tbsp **dried apricots, washed and quartered**
1 tbsp **dried papaya, washed and chopped**
1 tbsp **currants, washed**
1 tbsp **dates, roughly quartered**
1 tbsp **sunflower seeds**
1 tbsp **pumpkin seeds**
1 tbsp **banana chips**
1 tbsp **almonds, chopped**

What you do: Put all the ingredients in a large bowl. Mix together and store in an airtight jar. Serve with goat's, organic cow's, rice or soya milk, perhaps topped with a chopped banana or apple and a drizzle of honey.

Crunchy Nut Granola

Makes 1 lot: An excellent standby for when the munchies hit! Granola is a good way to start the day. Our blood sugar levels are very low in the mornings and the dried fruit in this recipe raises blood sugar and the grains help to sustain it. Some people prefer Granola without the dried fruit – do try it to see which you prefer. Granola is also excellent as a sweet, or pud, with some bio-live yoghurt and fruit. Cooking Granola is simple, you just need to keep an eye on it in the oven and take it out when it's golden.

What you need: 3 tbsp **sunflower oil**
3 tbsp **local honey**
2 cups **oat flakes**
2 cups **jumbo oat flakes**
1 tbsp **pumpkin seeds**
1 tbsp **almonds, chopped**
1 tbsp **brazil nuts, chopped**
1 tbsp **currants, washed**
1 tbsp **dates, washed and roughly quartered**
½ tbsp **dried papaya, chopped and washed**

What you do: Preheat the oven to 140°C/275°F/gas mark 1. Melt the honey and oil in a large saucepan on a gentle heat, being careful not to let the mixture come to the boil. When the honey has melted, remove the mixture from the heat. Add the remaining ingredients, minus the dried fruit. Stir and mix until well coated. Spread out on a large baking tray and pop into the oven for 30 minutes. Half way through the cooking, remove from the oven and mix thoroughly. Return to the oven. The granola is cooked when it is crisp and golden. Take out of the oven, stir to break up the lumps and allow to cool. Add the dried fruit and mix again. Store in an airtight container. Serve with your favourite milk as a breakfast or snack, or with some stewed fruit as a dessert.

Crunchy Nut Granola (page 32)

Smoothies (page 37). Vanilla – not the fast-food pissy kind, the real kind; and strawberry, our favourite.

Chips, Chips, glorious (Homemade) Chips (page 45)

Caesar Salad with Smokey Chicken (page 62)

'Sun'-Dried Tomatoes (page 41). If there were taste police, 'Sun'-Dried Tomatoes would be public enemy number one – they're that good!

Sweet Tomato and Basil Soup with Pesto Crostini (page 71)

Boiled Egg with Toasted Soldiers

Feeds 2: If you can tolerate eggs, this is an ideal way to start the day, full of power vitamins and minerals. And who can resist a boiled egg with toasted soldiers, the ridiculous and the sublime? Do try our variation, Coddled Egg, which is perfect comfort food for any age group.

What you need: 2 **free-range eggs**
4 slices **Soda Bread (page 143)**
2 knobs **organic butter**

What you do: Start by boiling 2 cups of water in a small saucepan. When bubbles appear, reduce the heat to a gentle simmer. Gently lower the first egg into the water on a tablespoon and do likewise with the second egg. Put the lid on and leave to cook for 3–4 minutes. Just before the eggs are ready, toast the Soda Bread until it's brown. Spread all four slices evenly with the butter and cut into soldiers. Gently take the eggs out of the pot and put into funky eggcups (we use shot glasses!). Serve at once with the toasted soldiers.

Coddled Egg

For Coddled Egg, use the same ingredients as for Boiled Egg with Toasted Soldiers. Proceed as above, but chop the toasted soldiers into squares. When the eggs are cooked, scoop the insides of both eggs out into 2 pretty cups, chop the mixture up a bit, add the toast squares, mix gently and season with a pinch of salt and a few twists of pepper. Tuck in at once.

Mexican Scrambled Eggs

Feeds 2: As well as a wonderful breakfast, scrambled egg makes a good snack. Not many people seem to be able to cook tasty scrambled egg, however, just a type of yellow rubber! Really it's very simple: just keep your nerve, and *don't* overcook it. When you think it's nearly done take the saucepan off the heat, the warmth of the saucepan will finish off the cooking. Anyway, I've never eaten *undercooked* scrambled egg, have you?

What you need: 1 slosh **extra virgin olive oil**
1 **scallion, chopped**
1 large **very ripe tomato, chopped into chunks**
2–3 **free-range eggs**
sea salt and freshly ground black pepper

4 slices **Soda Bread (page 143)**

What you do: In a heavy-bottomed saucepan, sauté the tomato and scallion in the butter and olive oil. Season generously. Cook on a medium heat for 4–5 minutes until the tomato is softish. Remove from the heat and allow to cool while you pop on your toast. Now add the eggs to the tomato and scallion mixture, mixing well so that the yolk and white combine. Put the saucepan back on the heat and cook slowly for 2 minutes, stirring so the egg doesn't stick to the sides of the saucepan or turn to rubber. A moment before the egg is cooked to your taste, take it off the heat – the warmth of the saucepan will finish the cooking. Serve at once with your soda toast.

Fried Tomatoes with Crispy Toast

Feeds 2: This is a warm, tasty breakfast at any time of the year – although we shouldn't eat too many tomatoes out of season, it's hard to resist. At the weekend when you have the time, try these tomatoes with Scrambled Egg, Sautéed Potatoes and a slice of fried bacon. Absolute indulgence.

What you need: 1 tbsp **extra virgin olive oil**
3 **very ripe tomatoes, sliced about 1 cm thick**
sea salt and freshly ground black pepper

4 slices **bread of your choice, for toast (see Excellent Breads pages 142–53)**

What you do: Warm the olive oil in a small frying pan. Add the tomato and season with a pinch of salt and lots of pepper. Cook on a medium heat – not too hot, as you don't want all the tomato juices evaporating. Cook for about 5 minutes until the tomato is soft on both sides. Meanwhile, toast the bread until nice and crispy.

Fried Bread

Feeds 4: Oh rapture, oh joy, oh damn this stuff is so very, very good. Not perhaps the very healthiest of dishes, but you will certainly enjoy it!

What you need: 1 tbsp **extra virgin olive oil**
30 g **organic butter**
2 slices **bread of your choice**

What you do: Put a pan on a medium heat and melt the butter. Add the bread to it. Make sure that you cover both sides of the bread evenly with the melted butter. Cook for 2 minutes, 1 minute each side, then add the olive oil and cook for a further 2 minutes, or until brown. Eat with A New Traditional breakfast or with Fried Tomatoes.

A New Traditional Breakfast

Feeds 4: This is a very strong recipe, so don't eat it when you are weak. Greasy foods are indeed bad, but this breakfast is sautéed in extra virgin olive oil and, provided you don't eat it for every meal, it's wonderful.

What you need:
4 tbsp **extra virgin olive oil**
3 **very ripe tomatoes, sliced about 1 cm thick**
4 slices **bacon**
3 large **boiled potatoes, sliced 1 cm thick**
3 **scallions, chopped**
4 **free-range eggs**
4 slices **bread of your choice**
sea salt and freshly ground black pepper

What you do: Cover the bottom of a large pan in the olive oil and put it on a medium heat. Arrange the potatoes in a single layer on the pan, then sprinkle with the chopped scallions. Season with a pinch of salt and lots of black pepper. Now get a second smaller pan, cover it in olive oil and spread the bacon out on the pan. Season the bacon with a few twists of pepper. Leave both pans to cook for 5 minutes. Add the tomatoes to the bacon pan – the oil the bacon is cooking in will make the tomato taste all the better. Turn the potatoes occasionally. Cook the bacon for a few more minutes or until brown. Then take the bacon off the pan on a plate and keep warm. Now gently squash the tomatoes (still in the pan) and season with salt and pepper. Leave the tomatoes for 3 more minutes, then take them off the pan and put them on the plate with the bacon. Take the potatoes off the pan and put them on the serving plate. Crack the eggs into the pan and fry to your taste. Take the eggs off the pan and put them on separate plates. Toast the bread till brown and serve at once.

Banana Smoothies

Makes 1: Smoothies could be considered the Green alternative to milkshakes, but I think that would be overestimating milkshakes and underestimating Smoothies. Smoothies are a fresh, sweet creamy (without cream) drink, suitable for a summer treat, a morning pick-me-up or when sugar cravings bite. Although we think that if you are having Smoothies for breakfast, it's best to only use bananas, you can use other fruit instead. Try mango, strawberries or any other soft fruit. Early in the morning, however, simplicity is always best.

What you need: ¾ cup **fresh banana or mango, or strawberries, prepared for eating**
¾ cup/188 ml **bio-live yoghurt or rice, oat or cow's milk**
honey, if desired

What you do: Put the fruit into a blender, add the milk and honey if using, and whizz. When completely smooth, pour into a tall glass with a few ice cubes. Serve and enjoy.

Yoghurt, Honey and Vanilla Smoothies

Makes 1: If you are dairy intolerant, it's best to avoid these Smoothies until your intolerance has levelled out a bit. That said, Chupi has always been dairy intolerant, but has never had a problem with organic bio-live natural yoghurt. Just try a little bit and see.

What you need: ½ cup/125 ml **apple juice, freshly pressed**
½ cup/125 ml **organic bio-live natural yoghurt**
2 tsp **local organic honey**
½ tsp **vanilla extract**

What you do: Whizz all the ingredients in a blender. Serve in a pretty glass.

Sautéed Potatoes with Chives

Feeds 4: Potatoes are the most wonderful food – fortifying, filling and delicious. Sautéed potatoes for breakfast really do set you up (until lunch!). Use good quality tatties, good olive oil, fresh herbs and scallions and you can't go wrong.

What you need:
3 tbsp **extra virgin olive oil**
4 large **boiled potatoes, cut into 1 cm slices**
3 **scallions, chopped**
1 tbsp **chives, finely chopped**
sea salt and freshly ground black pepper

What you do: Warm the olive oil in a large frying pan on a medium heat. Just as the oil starts to sizzle, pop on the potatoes. Arrange them in a single layer, sprinkle with the scallions and season well. Cook the potatoes for 7–8 minutes, turning occasionally. Season again with more pepper, sprinkle with the chopped chives and cook for a further minute until the potatoes are golden and crispy. Serve at once.

Pancakes with Sweet Honey and Bitter Lemon

Feeds 4: Our recipe is very similar to a 'normal' recipe for pancakes, we've just modified and replaced some of the ingredients. This is a good lesson if you find a recipe that looks appealing: just replace the things you can't have with things you can and the original flavour can usually be easily replicated. Try our pancakes which are healthy and tasty and see if you can spot the difference! I think lemon and honey is the best topping, though you can try thinly sliced banana and honey or Carob spread – a chocolate replacement, suitable for everyone, smeared over the pancakes. Delicious!

What you need: butter *or* sunflower oil
1¼ cups/188 g **white spelt *or* organic wheat flour**
2 **free-range eggs**
1½ cups/375 ml **rice, oat, soya, goat's *or* cow's milk**
2 tbsp **bio-live natural yoghurt**

3–4 tbsp **honey**
1 **lemon, cut into wedges**

What you do: Put the flour into a mixing bowl. Make a well in the centre, add the eggs. Gently mix, then slowly add the liquid and yoghurt, mixing with a balloon whisk. Keep gently whisking until a batter has formed. Leave the batter to stand for half an hour if you have the time. Put a non-stick pan, roughly 20 cm/8 in, on a high heat. When the pan is hot, put a knob of organic butter or drizzle of sunflower oil into it. Pour a ladleful of the batter onto the pan and swirl around until you have a pancake shape. Loosen the edges of the pancake with a knife. Cook for 2–3 minutes until bubbles form, then flip over and cook on the other side for a further 2–3 minutes. Take the pancake off the heat and keep in a warm place. Put another knob of butter or drizzle of oil into the pan and continue with the rest of the batter. Serve the pancakes with a tasty local honey and wedges of lemon.

Starters, Snacks, Sandwiches and Accompaniments

Although you can no longer fuel your frantic lifestyle with frantic food, while you adjust from one state of eating to another you will need – if you are to stick to the new regime – loads of tasty snacks to support your body and your mind. Practically all the recipes in this section are interchangeable. Most will make a gorgeous starter posh enough to serve to friends, an excellent snack when you are starving and a delicious sandwich or an accompaniment when you need a feast.

These are the recipes that will get you through.

'Sun'-Dried Tomatoes

Make 12 tomatoes: What does the image of sun-dried tomatoes conjure up? If all it brings to mind are small, leathery tomato halves drenched in vinegar and raw garlic and sold at exorbitant prices then you have been deceived. Proper sun-dried tomatoes are a treat – chopped up and mixed into pasta dishes, with salads and in sandwiches, they are a wow. They are also great if you're on a diet, as they add a caramelised sweetness to meals. Since we don't have consistently hot sun, here's how to cheat at 'sun'-dried tomatoes.

What you need: 6 **fresh, preferably on the vine, tomatoes**
3 cloves **garlic, whole with skins on**
2 tbsp **extra virgin olive oil**
few sprigs **fresh rosemary and thyme**
sea salt and freshly ground black pepper

What you do: Preheat the oven to 170°C/325°F/gas mark 3. Halve the tomatoes. Lie cut side down on a baking tray. Cover with lashings of olive oil, salt and pepper. Tuck the garlic cloves, rosemary and thyme between the tomatoes. Then pop into the oven and cook for roughly 1–1½ hours until they're dehydrated to your taste. If you're not going to use them all at once, you can store them in a clean, screw-top jar with a few chopped cloves of garlic, some more herbs and filled to the top with olive oil. Serve as a starter with Bruschetta, a snack with other snacks, as a very tasty ingredient in a sandwich, or as an accompaniment to savoury meals.

Slowly Roasted Garlic

Feeds 4: Garlic is gorgeous slowly roasted in its own skin as it turns super sweet and mellow. To release, just press down on the cooked cloves with the back of a fork and the hot, pungent garlic will come out. Serve as a starter or as an addition to (literally) any meal, with olive or other bread and some feta cheese. Give each person, for a starter, snack or accompaniment, ½–1 bulb of garlic each, depending on the size of both appetite and bulb of garlic.

What you need: ½ cup/125 ml **extra virgin olive oil**
2 bulbs of **garlic, whole and unpeeled**
few sprigs **rosemary, bay leaf and thyme**
sea salt and freshly ground black pepper

What you do: Preheat the oven to 230°C/450°F/gas mark 8. Tidy up the garlic bulbs by removing excess grotty bits, but be careful to leave the corm (the whole entire garlic) and the tightly bunched skins intact. Put into a roasting dish with the herbs and drizzle the olive oil over both bulbs. Season with lots of pepper and a pinch of salt. Pop into the oven for 20–30 minutes. Serve with a savoury bread and a lump of feta cheese.

Baked Tatties

Feeds 4: Baked potatoes, ah yummy baked potatoes – slowly roasted with their skins on, slit open and served with a knob of butter and sea salt , what could be better. For a more substantial meal, eat with Hummus, Slowly Roasted Garlic and salad.

What you need: 6–8 medium-large **'old' potatoes, unpeeled, scrubbed and cut in half**
4 cloves **garlic, not peeled**
few sprigs **rosemary and bay leaves**
2 tbsp **extra virgin olive oil**
1 **knob butter**
sea salt and freshly ground black pepper

What you do: Preheat the oven to 230°C/450°F/gas mark 8. Make sure the potatoes are well scrubbed. Put into a roasting tin with the olive oil, herbs and garlic. Season with lots of pepper and a little salt. Toss altogether so that the potatoes are well coated. Roast for approximately 1 hour – the exact cooking time depends on size, the bigger the potato the longer time it needs to cook. The potatoes are cooked when a knife or skewer slides easily in and the tatties themselves are beginning to feel soft when you press them gently. Serve sliced open with a knob of butter, a sprinkle of salt and the roasted garlic cloves.

Caspo Tatties

Feeds 4: Caspo Tatties are basically Baked Tatties with a gorgeous filling, rather rich, extremely tasty and good for cold evenings. We tend to eat them on their own, perhaps with a salad to fill in the corners.

What you need: 6 **large potatoes, scrubbed**
2 knobs **organic butter**
2 cloves **garlic, peeled and crushed**
2 **free-range eggs**
4 slices **parma ham chopped**
4 chunks **your favourite cheese (we use sheeps')**
2 tbsp **extra virgin olive oil**
4 **bay leaves**
sea salt and freshly ground black pepper

What you do: Preheat the oven to 230°C/450°F/gas mark 8. Put the potatoes, bay leaves and olive oil in a roasting tray, season with salt and pepper and toss to coat the potatoes. Place the tray in the oven and cook for 1 hour. While the potatoes are cooking, prepare the filling. Break the eggs into a large bowl, add the garlic, cheese, butter and ham. Season with salt and pepper and mix together. When the potatoes are cooked, take the tray out of the oven, cut the potatoes in half and scoop out the flesh, being careful not to damage the skins. Add the potato flesh to the bowl and mix everything together. Scoop the mixture back into the potato skins. Push the potato halves back together, return to the oven and roast for a further 5–10 minutes. Serve with a Green Salad.

Homemade Chips

Feeds 4: Chips, chips, glorious chips, a fine accompaniment to any meal, or delicious as snack on their own. Just one thing: when you're making chips do use a good sunflower oil. Other oils just aren't worth using, as many contain genetically modified ingredients.

What you need: 6 large **rooster potatoes**
1 l good quality **sunflower oil**
sea salt and freshly ground black pepper

What you do: Make sure you have a heavy pot (it's safer, as it is far less likely to tip over), with a well-fitting lid. Fill the pot two-thirds up with good quality sunflower oil and put on a high heat. While the oil is heating, peel the potatoes and slice into chips, roughly the width of your index finger. Your oil should be hot enough by now. To test it, drop in a chip – if it sizzles vigorously, the oil is ready. Tip the chips into the oil, being very careful to avoid any spitting, cook for 15–20 minutes or until golden brown. Remove the cooked chips with a slotted spoon to drain on a plate spread with kitchen paper. Sprinkle with salt, and *voilà*.

Cheese and Bacon Chips
Ohhhh! Oww! The food just gets better and better…! This is Luke's delicious fast-food topping for Chips.

4 **pieces organic bacon, chopped**
4 **scallions, chopped**
Cheddar cheese (organic if possible) *or* **feta**
Harissa (page 160) *or* **chilli powder**
sea salt and freshly ground black pepper

First, get the chips cooking as above. While they are cooking, put the bacon and scallions in a pan with a slosh of olive oil. Cook gently on a medium heat until the bacon is cooked through, say 7–9 minutes. Remove from heat. When the chips are cooked, dry them in a bowl lined with kitchen paper. Remove kitchen paper. Top the chips with the cooked bacon and scallions. Grate cheese or feta directly onto the warm chips. Drizzle with Harissa, or sprinkle with chilli. Season with salt and black pepper. Gently stir to mix all the ingredients together. Serve. (For best friends only.)

Tuna, Mayo and Cucumber Sambos

Feeds 4: Tuna and mayo sandwiches are so good, we used to eat them all the time when we were little. The first summer we grew cucumbers, we had to find a delicious way of using them. Then Tara came up with this great idea – the cucumber reduces the oiliness of the fish, and with homemade mayo you'll want to eat more and more …

1 tin **tuna in sunflower oil**

The Mayonnaise

What you need: 1 **egg yolk**
½ cup/125 ml **extra virgin olive oil**
¼ cup/62 ml **sunflower oil**
a good squeeze **fresh lemon juice**
1 small **cucumber, chopped**
4 **scallions, finely chopped**
sea salt and freshly ground black pepper

4 **Farls, cut in half (page 146)**

2 handfuls **salad leaves**

What you do: For the mayonnaise, combine the two oils, then get a small bowl and put the egg yolk into it. Start by adding the first drop of oil, gently mixing it into the yolk. Add the second drop and mix in, always making sure to combine the last drop of oil before adding the next. Slowly increase the amount of oil, but be careful and don't add too much at a time or it's bound to curdle. When the egg has absorbed all the oil, add the lemon juice. Season with salt and pepper to taste. Now combine the mayo, tuna, cucumber and scallions in a bowl and mix gently but thoroughly. Season with a pinch of salt and lots of black pepper. Divide the mixture into quarters and spread over each half Farl. Add some salad leaves to each sandwich, pop on the tops, season again and eat.

Panzerotte

Makes 6: Panzerotte are so versatile, they fulfil all parts of this section: they can be served as a starter, a snack or a sandwich and are especially good for picnics as everything is sealed tight. Pulled apart, they emit wonderful smells of whatever delicious filling you've chosen, but do make sure that the filling is good and intense, with loads of herbs, spices, olive oil, salt and pepper.

What you need: ½ cup/75 g **white spelt** *or* **organic wheat flour**
½ tsp **bread soda**
1 tbsp **bio-live organic natural yoghurt**
2 tbsp **extra virgin olive oil**
½ tbsp **your chosen herbs, chopped**
sea salt and freshly ground black pepper

The Filling
organic feta cheese
rosemary, chopped, *or*
Spinach Frittata (page 48)
organic soft cheese, *or*
courgette mixture from Zucchini Pasta (page 83)
organic goat's cheese, *or*
very ripe tomato, chopped
parma ham or cooked bacon, chopped
hard organic cheese, grated *or*
Feta and Sage Relish (page 157)

What you do: Preheat the oven to 230°C/450°F/gas mark 8. Mix the flour and bread soda in a bowl. Add the yoghurt and enough water to make a dry, pliable dough. Split the dough into 6 pieces and roll each into a squarish circle not more than .5 cm thick. Put a large tbsp of your chosen mix of ingredients into the middle of each circle, season generously and add some chopped up herbs – basil and rosemary are our favourites – and a good drizzle of extra virgin olive oil. Fold each circle in half and pinch the pastry together to form half-moons. Glaze with more olive oil. Put into the oven for 10–15 minutes or until the parcels are golden brown. Serve with a Green Salad.

Spinach Frittata

Feeds 4: If Sunday morning arrives and you're looking for a tasty brunch, look no further. Frittata are Italian omelettes and you can fill them with anything you choose. They look very impressive too, while being simplicity itself to make. They can be served as a starter, a snack or with a Green Salad as a main meal. And they are a great way to get reluctant spinach eaters started.

What you need: 400 g **spinach**
1 knob **organic butter**
2 tbsp **extra virgin olive oil**
6 **tomatoes, chopped**
6–8 **free-range eggs**
2 chunks **organic feta goat's cheese**
sea salt and freshly ground black pepper

What you do: To sauté the spinach: put the spinach, butter and 1 tbsp of the oil into a saucepan on a medium heat with lots of pepper and a pinch of salt. Stir to make sure the spinach is coated, pop on the lid and leave for 4 minutes. Stir again. Now continue cooking until the spinach has reduced by roughly half (this should take 8 minutes at the most). Meanwhile, pop the tomatoes and 1 tbsp of the oil into a small, heavy-bottomed frying pan or saucepan. Cook on a medium heat for 4–5 minutes, stirring occasionally. The tomato and spinach should 'arrive' at about the same time. Put the tomato to one side while you cook the frittata. Method one: heat a medium-sized, heavy-bottomed frying pan. Drizzle with olive oil and add the beaten eggs. Allow to set (roughly 30 seconds). Now spread the spinach over the egg mixture and allow to cook until the egg is done to your taste (we like ours just firm, about 3 minutes). Method two: use a very small, heavy-bottomed frying pan and cook a quarter of the spinach and egg at a time for individual frittatas. Otherwise you can cut the large frittata into quarters. To serve, take four pretty plates and put one frittata or one quarter of the large frittata on to each plate and top with one quarter of the fried tomato and a chunk of cheese. Season generously.

The Perfect Goat's Cheese, Salad and Tomato Sandwich

Feeds 2: It's so simple to make a sandwich – just stuff lots of yummy ingredients inside two pieces of bread and scoff. When you can't eat wheat or yeast it is absolutely impossible to get a decent sandwich: sourdough is too bitter and soda just crumbles. That's why I urge you to try our Farls (page 146), as they make what is a fantastic sandwich sublime. If you can't tolerate cheese of any sort, try this sandwich with either Mayonnaise (page 159) or a few slices of ripe avocado as a replacement.

What you need: 2 **Farls (page 146) or 4 pieces bread**
1 **tomato, very thinly sliced**
a few **very thin slices red onion**
2 large chunks **hard goat's cheese, or your favourite organic cheddar, sliced**
8–10 **green salad leaves**
extra virgin olive oil
sea salt and freshly ground black pepper

What you do: Slice the Farls in half and lightly toast. Meanwhile, prepare the tomato and onion. Split the filling between the two sandwiches. Start with a layer of cheese, then the tomato, then the onion. Season generously. Drizzle the sandwich with some olive oil. Top with the salad leaves and sandwich top. Eat at once, or pack up for picnicking later.

Quickie Pizzas

Feeds 4: There's something about pizza that nothing else quite replicates. But pizza does take a certain amount of work, so here are some Quickie Pizzas perfect as a snack, a quick lunch or a mid-evening filler. They don't take as much time or energy as normal pizza, but you still get that lovely pizza hit.

What you need: 2 **Farls (page 146), sliced open**
4 **very ripe tomatoes, thinly sliced**
1 **red onion, sliced paper-thin**
enough **organic mature cheddar,** or **feta, to cover the pizzas**
1 tbsp mixed **fresh rosemary, basil and parsley, finely chopped**
2–3 tbsp **extra virgin olive oil**
sea salt and freshly ground black pepper

What you do: Pre-heat the oven 150°C/350°F/gas mark 4. Slice the Farls open to get 4 separate pizzas, pop into the toaster for a minute or two to crisp up. On the cut side, layer the tomatoes, then the onions and then the cheese. Season generously with olive oil, freshly ground black pepper and sea salt. Pop into the oven for 10 minutes. Remove from the oven and serve hot. You can serve these as a main meal with a Green Salad (page 61) to fill up the corners.

Different toppings

Our favourite pizza is definitely a Margarita, so it is no surprise that the above is topped with a quick imitation of that pizza. You can, however, use other toppings, say **6–8 slices parma ham** underneath the tomato layer for a meat version of the above. You could try **Spinach Frittata (page 48)** spread across the base, topped with **feta cheese** or 6 tbsp **crème fraiche**, cooked as above. The only limit is your imagination.

A Mexican Snack:
Guacamole and Nachos

Feeds 4: Guacamole and Nachos are such a classic combination that it seems obvious to join them together as a starter or as a snack. We make our own nachos as it's so simple. One note on the different varieties of avocado: you can usually buy two varieties, the tastiest of which is Hass, with its 'warty', nearly black skin. It tastes miles better than its watery green relation.

What you need: 1 **good-sized, ripe avocado, peeled, stoned and chopped**
1 clove **garlic, peeled and crushed**
a small squeeze **lemon juice, freshly squeezed**
sea salt and freshly ground black pepper

1 quantity Tortillas (page 144) *or* 1 bag suitable Nachos

What you do: You need to make the Nachos first, so put a pan on to warm, cover with a thin layer of olive oil and get the Tortillas. Cut each Tortilla straight down the middle so you have 2 half-moons. Then halve each half-moon so you have four quadrants. Then halve each quadrant so you have 8 triangles in all. You should now have 8 uncooked Nachos per Tortilla. The pan should be hot enough by now, so pop 1 Tortilla worth of Nachos onto the pan and fry for a minute or 2 each side or until golden. Remove to drain on kitchen paper. Continue with the rest of the Tortillas. Meanwhile, roughly mash the chopped up avocado, garlic and small squeeze of lemon with a fork. We like guacamole quite chunky, but some people prefer a more puréed consistency; try both and you'll find the consistency you prefer. Season generously. Serve as a dip with the nachos and perhaps some Zingy Tomato Salsa (page 158), as part of a group of salads, or as an element of a sandwich filling.

Grown-up Guacamole
Guacamole is suitable for everyone as served above, but if you want to enliven it a bit you can add **1 very ripe tomato, finely chopped** and **2 scallions, finely chopped** to the recipe. Serve as above.

Bruschetta

Makes 8 pieces: With all the dips in this section, it's important to have something good to eat them with. Bruschetta are the perfect solution. A sort of upmarket fried bread, Bruschetta are goldenly crisp and perfect for scooping up Hummus, Avocado Hummus, Broad Bean Purée or Guacamole. Bruschetta is traditionally made with a white yeast bread, but we've used brown soda – both shop-bought and homemade – with success. However, if you want to be both Green and traditional, use a white spelt or organic wheat, sourdough. You can up the quantities if it's for a big feed or for a party, but I'm guessing these quantities are to serve four people as a robust starter.

What you need: 2 tbsp **extra virgin olive oil**
3 cloves **garlic, crushed**
4 slices **bread of your choice (see Excellent Breads pages 142–53)**

What you do: Lightly toast the bread. Rub both sides of the toasted bread with the crushed garlic and olive oil. Presentation is everything so you can either serve the Bruschetta piled on a plate with bowls of Hummus, Avocado Hummus, Broad Bean Purée and Guacamole with some crudités (such as carrots, celery etc. cut into pretty sticks for dipping and to contrast with the Bruschetta). Or you could cut each Bruschetta in half, pile each half with your chosen dip and top with a suitable garnish.

Lemon Millet Tabouleh

Feeds 4: Most Taboulehs are made with couscous. Couscous is not in fact a grain, but rolled wheat, which is not very good if you're wheat intolerant. Millet is a wonderful grain, acceptable for people who are wheat and even gluten intolerant. Do try this tabouleh as a tasty snack, starter, accompaniment to a meal with a large salad, as a pasta replacement or with a chicken breast as a main meal.

What you need: ¾ cup **millet grain**
1¼ cup/312 ml **Veggie Stock (page 69)**
1 tbsp **flat-leaf parsley, chopped**
3 **scallions, finely chopped**
3 tbsp **extra virgin olive oil**
2 tbsp **lemon juice, fresh**
2 cloves **garlic, peeled and crushed**

What you do: Put the millet and stock into a saucepan with a tight-fitting lid. Cook on a medium heat for 15–20 minutes or until the millet is cooked and fluffy. Mix with the rest of the ingredients. Serve warm or cold.

Japanese Tempura Vegetables

Feeds 4: Tempura are vegetables in batter, deep-fried. It may sound bizarre, but Tempura is so good – the veg is gorgeous, crisp on the outside, sweet on the inside. This is an excellent way to encourage vegetable eating. We eat Tempura with something simple, but remember to include plenty of dips, perhaps Aioli (page 159), Harrisa (page 160), or Guacamole (page 51). Tempura can serve as a starter, snack or whole meal, provided you have a mix of salads alongside. Gram flour is a wonderful flour, made from chickpeas and suitable for coeliacs, so do make an effort to find it (try your local health food store). For the vegetables, you can also include whatever are in season.

What you need: 1 cup/150 g **gram (chickpea) flour**
½ cup/125 ml **water**
1 **free-range egg white, beaten until fluffy**
10 sprigs **broccoli, broken into florets**
2 **carrots, topped and tailed, unpeeled if organic, cut into sticks**
8 **runner** or **green beans, topped, tailed and halved**
1 small **courgette, cut into 3 cm sticks**
sunflower oil for deep-frying
ground cumin and coriander (optional)
sea salt and freshly ground black pepper

What you do: Put the oil into a pan on a medium-high heat. Prepare the vegetables. For the batter: mix the flour and water, whisk to remove any lumps, then gently fold in the egg white. Season with lots of pepper and a pinch of sea salt. You could add 1 tsp each ground cumin and coriander if you would like to spice it up. Chuck all the veg into the batter. Mix well, ensuring it's all well coated. The oil should be hot by now, so put roughly half the veg into the oil. Cook for 5–6 minutes, stirring once or twice, until lightly golden. Remove from the oil with a slotted spoon and drain on kitchen paper. Repeat with the remaining tempura. Serve at once with plenty of dips.

Onion Bhajis

Makes 6–8 bhajis: Onion Bhajis are another triumph of India's extraordinary culinary classics, but beware, they are quite intense and not to be gorged on if your system is sensitive. As a snack or starter with a few dips, or as an accompaniment to an Indian meal, they're supreme. A small tip when cooking: remember always to use a good oil; we use sunflower.

What you need: 1 cup/150 g **gram (chickpea) flour**
½ tsp each **cumin, fennel, black mustard and coriander seeds, coarsely crushed**
1 tsp each **ground cumin, ground coriander and turmeric**
1 **onion, peeled and finely chopped**
1 **potato, peeled and grated**
½ cup/125 ml **water**
sea salt and freshly ground black pepper

A saucepan filled with 6 cm depth of sunflower oil

What you do: Put the oil on a medium-high heat while you prepare the recipe. Combine the flour and spices in a bowl. Slowly add the water to make a smooth batter, then add in the prepared onions and potato. Season generously. Mix well. Drop one tablespoon of the thickish mixture into the hot oil, or more depending on the size of your saucepan. It's fine if the bhajis bump together as they cook, but you don't want them so tightly packed they form one big goo. Cook for 5–8 minutes until golden brown. Remove and drain on kitchen paper. Repeat until all the mixture is used.

Two Different Hummus

Makes 1 lot: We've two different kinds of Hummus here, as each is delicious in its own way. Original Hummus is absolute heaven when made properly. A bowl of Hummus and a few Bruschetta – give me 5 minutes and there will be nothing left! Avocado Hummus is Original Hummus with the addition of an avocado.

What you need: 1 tin **chickpeas**
2 cloves **garlic, peeled and crushed**
a small squeeze **lemon juice, freshly squeezed**
pinch of **cayenne pepper**
1 tbsp **mild tahini**
sea salt and freshly ground black pepper

Nachos, Bruschetta, Crudités

What you do: Just whizz all the ingredients to a roughish consistency and scrape out into a pretty bowl. Season generously and garnish with a pinch of cayenne pepper. Serve as a dip, starter or sandwich filling with Nachos (page 51), Bruschetta (page 52) or crudités.

Avocado Hummus
Add 1 good-sized **ripe avocado, peeled and stoned** just before you whizz the Original Hummus. Serve as above.

Cheese-Butty Chilli Sarnies

Feeds 2: This is Luke's recipe, so when we debated whether or not this should be a one- or two-person affair, he had the deciding vote: 'It's so damn good you could cook for two and eat it alone.' So here it is, Luke's version of the traditional toasted cheese with a new twist. Luke thinks this recipe is best served with a glass of beer, or failing that a glass of apple juice. On the subject of bread, we use homemade, but shop-bought is OK if you can tolerate dairy and wheat. Or you could use your favourite bread, provided it meets the green requirements. You can also eat these without the bacon, though Luke would not approve.

What you need:
1 tbsp **extra virgin olive oil**
4 **scallions, chopped**
3 **rashers of bacon, cut into strips**
1 large or 2 small **very ripe tomatoes, sliced**
2 slices **bread, 1 cm thick (see Excellent Breads pages 142–53)**
organic mature cheddar, or feta (to cover bread)
1 tsp **Harissa (page 160) or other chilli sauce**
freshly ground black pepper

What you do:

Place a frying pan on a medium heat with a slosh of olive oil. Fry the bacon and scallions for 7–8 minutes, or until browned. Meanwhile, lightly toast the bread. Cover with cheese, sliced tomato and a sprinkle of chilli. Season each slice with lots of pepper (no salt is necessary as the bacon will provide). Pop the breads under the grill until the cheese has melted and the tomato is soft, around 5–6 minutes. Remove, divide the cooked bacon between the two slices and dribble a teaspoon of Harissa over each. Serve at once with a Green Salad if you want to make a meal of it. Mouth wateringly delish!

Salads

Luckily the time has passed when all you got when you ordered a green salad was some limp lettuce and raw tomato. There is nothing more scrumptious than a good salad, the perfect accompaniment to any meal, reaching every single cell in the body. For Green salad, grow your own in window boxes, visit your local country market, get stuck into your local organic farm, do whatever it takes to get good leaves – these are the heart of your salad. Unless, of course, you're trying one of our tasty bean salads. Either way, salads are an excellent companion to all meals or a good stand-alone snack.

Mixed Bean Salad with Olive Oil Dressing

Feeds 4: Bean Salad, another wholefood staple and very tasty. We tend to eat Bean Salad as part of an array of salads. Originally this would have been made with home-cooked beans, but we feel it's too much work! If you have the time to cook the beans, there is a taste difference, but good tinned beans are perfectly acceptable. Bean Salad does benefit from being left to marinate for a while.

What you need: 1 tin **organic mixed beans**
1 cup **bean sprouts**
½ cup/125 ml **extra virgin olive oil**
1 clove **garlic, peeled and crushed**
a good squeeze **fresh lemon juice**
sea salt and freshly ground black pepper

What you do: Rinse the beans, then toss them with the rest of the ingredients. Season generously. Serve with Green Salad and a baked potato.

Goat's Cheese and Roasted Vegetable Salad

Feeds 2: We first made this recipe as summer was turning into autumn and the need for a warm salad – something which feels daft during the summer – emerged. It's very simple: chop up, drizzle, bung in the oven, eat. You can also barbecue the veg if there's enough sunshine and you have the inclination. Very simple, suitable for everyone, sensitive or otherwise.

What you need:
2 tbsp **extra virgin olive oil**
6 cloves **garlic, unpeeled and whole**
2 large **very ripe tomatoes, quartered**
1 **red pepper, deseeded and cut into 12 strips**
1 **courgette, halved widthways and cut into thick sticks**
few sprigs **fresh rosemary, bay leaves**
2 **scallions, chopped in half**
sea salt and freshly ground black pepper

lots of **lettuce and mixed salad leaves**
a lump **organic feta**
1 handful **fresh basil leaves, torn**
2 tbsp **extra virgin olive oil**

What you do: Preheat the oven to 230°C/450°F/gas mark 8. Place the garlic, tomatoes, pepper, courgette and herbs into an ovenproof dish. Drizzle with the olive oil and season generously. Pop into the oven and roast for 15 minutes. Remove from the oven, add the scallions and toss. Then put back into the oven for a further 10–15 minutes or until the vegetables are cooked. Meanwhile, mix the remainder of the olive oil with the basil. When the vegetables are cooked, toss them with the olive oil and serve on top of the salad leaves, crumbled with the feta.

Green Salad with Toasted Pumpkin Seeds

Feeds 4: A good Green Salad is excellent as a starter, as an accompaniment to a big meal, or as part of an array of food such as Lentil Soup and a Baked Potato for a super-delicious and nourishing meal. A note about buying salad greens: always buy organic, or even better grow your own. Salads can be easily grown in a container indoors or out – and you will know what's happened to your lettuce. Pumpkin seeds with salad might sound strange, but they are delicious, so give them a try!

What you need: 1 good-sized tbsp **pumpkin seeds**
½ **cos lettuce**
a generous selection different salad leaves, e.g. **oakleaf, lollo rosso**
a few (5–10) leaves **red radicchio** (to add colour)

What you do: To toast the pumpkin seeds you can either use the oven or a dry frying pan. For the oven: preheat it to 250°C/475°F/gas mark 9. Put the pumpkin seeds on a tray and pop into the oven for 5 minutes while you prepare the salad. For the pan: dry fry the pumpkin seeds in a frying pan for 4–5 minutes, until lightly browned and crispy. Wash the salad leaves well, shake off the excess water and roughly chop or tear. Put into a serving bowl. When the pumpkin seeds are done, pop them into the bowl with the salad. Serve the salad on its own or with a dressing (page 64) as a stand-alone snack, starter or accompaniment to a main meal.

Caesar Salad with Smokey Chicken

Feeds 4: This recipe came about when after preparing and cooking the separate parts of Chicken Sarnies we decided we wanted something more green! So we put the chicken and mayo into a serving bowl with loads of salad leaves and a chunk of bread to mop up the juices. This is a somewhat complicated recipe, but it's so divine and looks so good it's worth it.

The Chicken

What you need:
2 tbsp **extra virgin olive oil**
4 **scallions, chopped**
3 good-sized **chicken breasts, sliced into 1 cm strips**
2 cloves **garlic, peeled and crushed**
1 tbsp **fresh rosemary and parsley, chopped**
sea salt and freshly ground black pepper

The Salad

What you need:
½ **cos lettuce**
a generous selection different lettuces, e.g. **oakleaf, lollo rosso**
1 **scallion, chopped**
a chunk **organic feta** or **similar cheese, chopped**
2 tbsp **organic bio-live natural yoghurt**

The Dressing

What you need:
1 **free-range egg yolk**
½ cup/125 ml **extra virgin olive oil**
½ cup/125 ml **bio-live natural yoghurt**
1 clove **garlic, peeled and crushed**
a good squeeze **fresh lemon juice**
sea salt and freshly ground black pepper

What you do: Put all the prepared chicken ingredients into a large frying pan on a medium heat and season generously. The chicken will take about 12–15 minutes, with occasional stirring to prevent sticking, but if you keep an eye on it you can let it do its own thing while you prepare the salad and dressing. For the dressing, get a small bowl and put the egg yolk into it. Start by adding the first drop of oil, gently mixing it into the yolk. Add the second drop and mix in again, making sure to combine the last drop of oil before adding the next. Slowly increase the amount of oil, but take it slowly or it will curdle. When the egg has absorbed all the oil, add the lemon juice and yoghurt. Season with salt and pepper to taste. The chicken should be just cooked, so pop it into a serving dish on the table along with the salad ingredients and the dressing and mix it all together. A Farl (page 146) or Cheese and Chive Scone (page 148) is an excellent accompaniment to this salad.

A Basic Salad Dressing

Makes 1 jar: If you've ever read a list of ingredients for the average salad dressing, or tasted the vinegary goo dolloped over wilted lettuce, then you'll appreciate our perky, tasty dressing for your salads or even to pep your foods up. These dressings can also be stored in the fridge for a few days.

What you need: 1 tbsp **lemon juice, freshly squeezed**
1 cup/250 ml **extra virgin olive oil**
sea salt and freshly ground black pepper

What you do: Pour the olive oil into a jug, add the lemon juice and season generously. Whisk lightly before serving. Pop on to the table and everyone can drizzle their own.

Different Dressings

The basic dressing is very tasty, but sometimes it's good to have different tastes.

For a **Herb Dressing**, add 1 tbsp **mixed parsley, rosemary, chives and mint, chopped**, to the basic dressing.

For a **Honey and Garlic Dressing**, add 1 **clove of garlic, crushed** and 2 tbsp **local honey** to the basic dressing, or to the herb dressing.

Blazing Salads Soup (page 72), probably the best soup in the world

Zucchini Pasta, the Italian connection (page 83)

The Ultimate Veggie Burger (page 92). It's hard to believe that paradise comes in pieces this small!

Spelt Pasta with Broad Beans, Tomatoes and Goat's Cheese (page 88)

Chupi and Luke in Temple Bar food market, Dublin, vegging out

Chupi and Luke scoffing Quickie Pizza (page 50)

Butter Bean, Sun-dried Tomato and Basil Salad

Feeds 4: This is our interpretation of a very tasty salad we had in a Dublin restaurant, though without the vinegar. If you have the time to cook the butter beans from scratch, do – there is a taste difference – but good, organic tinned beans are perfectly acceptable. This is lovely served with a few other salads, as an accompaniment or tossed through freshly cooked pasta.

What you need:
1 tin **organic butter beans**
6–8 **sun-dried tomatoes (page 41), finely chopped**
1 tbsp **fresh basil, roughly chopped**
1 tbsp **extra virgin olive oil**
1 clove **garlic, peeled and crushed**
a good squeeze **fresh lemon juice**
sea salt and freshly ground black pepper

What you do: Rinse the beans well if tinned, as you need to get rid of the goo they were preserved in. Combine all the ingredients in a pretty bowl. If possible, leave the salad to marinate for a while. Serve at room temperature.

Tuna, Mayo and Fennel Salad

Feeds 4: A tuna salad is wonderful, so filling and sustaining. This bears no comparison to the normal tuna fish salad, which is made of horrible tuna, cheap mayonnaise and tinned sweet corn; it is a breath of fresh air, with its crisp cucumber and fennel to cut through the mayonnaise. It's not really an accompaniment, but is best served with some crispy bread as a light lunch.

What you need: 1 tin **tuna in sunflower oil**
1 **egg yolk**
½ cup/125 ml **extra virgin olive oil**
¼ cup/62 ml **sunflower oil**
a good squeeze **fresh lemon juice**
1 small **cucumber, sliced**
1 bulb **fennel, thinly sliced**
4 **scallions, chopped**
sea salt and freshly ground black pepper

a bowl **salad leaves**
2 **Farls (page 146)**

What you do: To make the mayo combine the two oils. Get a small bowl and put the egg yolk into it. Start by adding the first drop of oil gently mixing it into the yolk. Add the second drop, mix in again, as usual making sure to combine the last drop of oil before adding the next. When the egg has absorbed all the oil, add the lemon juice. Season with salt and pepper to taste. Now combine the tuna, cucumber, fennel and scallions in a bowl and mix gently but thoroughly. Season again. Serve on a bed of salad leaves with some crispy bread – say a toasted Farl.

Avocado, Tomato and Extra Virgin Olive Oil Salad

Feeds 4: With some cooking you can afford to not use the best ingredients, but not in salads. Make sure the avocadoes are ripe, and try to find the Hass variety (nearly black in colour). The difference in flavour is incredible. You also need to use on-the-vine tomatoes that are perfectly ripe and a really fruity extra virgin olive oil.

What you need: 2 small *or* 1 large **ripe avocado, peeled, stoned and chopped**
2 **very ripe tomatoes, chopped**
1 **scallion, very finely chopped**
1 clove **garlic, peeled and crushed**
3 tbsp **extra virgin olive oil**
sea salt and freshly ground black pepper

What you do: Gently mix all the ingredients together. Season generously with salt and pepper. Serve on its own or as a stand-alone snack, starter or accompaniment to a main meal.

Carrot Salad with a Squeeze of Lemon

Feeds 4: This is a tasty, simple salad, very popular in wholefood restaurants. We eat it with a selection of other salads when we feel like what a friend calls 'pure rabbit food'.

What you need: 3 **carrots, peeled and grated**
1 tbsp **flaked almonds**
1 large squeeze **lemon juice, freshly squeezed**
1 tbsp **extra virgin olive oil**

What you do: Simply mix all the ingredients together. Serve as an accompaniment or with other salads, perhaps a Green Salad.

Soups

When you're sensitive, soup is the best food: gentle on the digestive system and yet, if properly prepared, 'a meal in a bowl'. Using this principle, we recommend extras to serve with the soups for a proper meal, just add or take away whatever you fancy. Making your own stock is a must. Most bought stock cubes are MSG, wheat, yeast, salt and additive laden, a lethal cocktail for the body. But don't worry, getting a stock pot together is really easy; once you have it up and going, delicious soups will be the order of the day.

Veggie Stock

Makes approx. 1 litre: The key to good soups (apart from buying the best and, as far as possible, organic, ingredients) is the stock; a good homemade stock is a must for those of us with food sensitivities. MSG (monosodium glutamate), the flavour enhancer used in most stock cubes and in hundreds of processed foods, is hell on a sensitive system. Making your own stock might seem like a Victorian impossibility – in reality it's easy. The bonus is that once you have a stockpot started, you can just keep adding to it as you go along.

What you need:
2 **onions (with skin still on) chopped in half**
1 **leek, chopped in half**
1 **large carrot**
2–3 **outer leaves cabbage**
2–3 **winter/spring greens**
1 stick **celery/several leaves lovage**
2 cloves **garlic (with skin still on), chopped in half**
1 **bouquet garni (bay leaves/thyme/parsley/sage/rosemary)**
1.5 l **water**

What you do: Scrub your vegetables and remove any grotty bits. Put them all into a medium-sized saucepan with a tight-fitting lid. Cover in cold water, bring to the boil and let it simmer away merrily while you make the soup (a good stock needs a minimum of 30 minutes to get all the flavours from the veg). Be creative, use whatever veggies are seasonal and to hand. Your stock pot, if kept in a cold place, will last up to 10 days with you adding more vegetables to keep up the intensity of the flavour.

Young Broad Bean and Creamy Yoghurt Soup

Feeds 4: Soups are so simple and easy, we tend to live off them during winter when all you want is warm comfort food. However, Broad Bean Soup is best eaten midsummer, as the first tender broad beans arrive into our shops and it can be eaten all the way into early autumn. Broad beans are at their best when they're young, but if you can only get the ancient leathery variety, peel the tough grey outer skin after they're cooked – a labour of love, but worth it if you have the time and patience!

What you need: 3 cups **broad beans, de-podded**
1 tbsp **extra virgin olive oil**
1 **onion, peeled and chopped**
2 cloves **garlic, peeled and crushed**
5 cups/1.25 l **Veggie Stock (page 69)**
sea salt and freshly ground black pepper

1 tbsp **fresh parsley**
1 tbsp **fresh organic bio-live natural yoghurt**

What you do: Sauté the onion and garlic in the olive oil for 6–8 minutes or until soft. Add the beans. Cook for 1–2 minutes. Add the stock to the onions, garlic, and beans. (Now, if you want to, you can use a cup of yoghurt in place of 1 cup of stock.) Season generously. When cooked, whizz until smooth. Put the saucepan back on the heat and cook for a further 5 minutes to reduce the stock. Serve in 4 bowls with a dollop of yoghurt and a sprinkle of parsley. This is a very delicate soup, so I'd go without bread, but you could have a Cheese and Chive Scone (page 148) as an accompaniment.

Sweet Tomato and Basil Soup with Pesto Crostini

Feeds 4: Every recipe we've ever read for tomato soup agrees that without liberal quantities of sugar to counteract the acidity of the tomatoes the soup is not worth making; we disagree! If the soup is properly cooked, the tomatoes release their own flavour, making a very sweet soup indeed. Though we find tomato soup quite strong, one small bowl and a heap of pesto crostini make a very acceptable meal, especially in the hot summer sun.

What you need: 2 tbsp **extra virgin olive oil**
1 clove **garlic, peeled and crushed**
1 **onion, peeled and chopped**
2 tins **tomatoes, chopped**
1 tbsp **fresh basil**
1 cup/250 ml **Veggie Stock (page 69)**
1 tbsp **organic bio-live natural yoghurt**
sea salt and freshly ground black pepper

1 quantity **Bruschetta (page 52)**
½ quantity **Green Basil Pesto (page 161)**

What you do: Warm the olive oil in a heavy-bottomed saucepan on a medium heat. Sauté the onion and garlic for 5–6 minutes without allowing to brown. Add the tomatoes, stock and basil. Stir. Season generously. Leave to cook for 10 minutes on a simmering heat. A few minutes before the soup is cooked make the Bruschetta. Smear each Bruschetta with a large dollop of the Green Basil Pesto. Remove the soup from the heat and blend to a smooth consistency. Return to the heat, add the yoghurt and warm to serving temperature. Then serve in 4 beautiful bowls with 2 Pesto Crostini beside each.

Blazing Salads Soup

Feeds 4: Lentil soup, for that is what this recipe is, may not seem all that inspiring, but it is wonderfully gentle comfort food. Very subtle, it's perfect when you are very sensitive. Lentil soup is also wonderful because, stalwart of vegetarians for decades, most meat eaters – who wouldn't normally dream of eating anything veggie – will happily scoff this! In the notes on this recipe there's attempt No. 1 with the words 'Disaster, even the dogs wouldn't touch it' and then attempt No. 2 'Yay!' Here's No. 2, dedicated in loving memory to that gem Blazing Salads, the best alternative restaurant in Dublin and a saviour when all other food avenues were dark.

What you need:
2 tbsp **extra virgin olive oil**
2 cloves **garlic, peeled and crushed**
1 large **onion, peeled and chopped**
1 cup **red lentils**
1 **carrot, peeled and chopped**
1 tsp each **ground cumin and coriander**
1 tbsp **fresh rosemary and parsley, chopped**
5 cups/1.25 l **water** *or* **Veggie Stock (page 69)**
sea salt and freshly ground black pepper

Cheese and Chive Scones (page 148)

What you do: Put the onion, garlic, carrot and olive oil into a saucepan on a medium heat. Sauté for 7–8 minutes without allowing them to brown. Now add the lentils, spices, herbs and stock. Season generously. Bring to the boil then reduce the heat. Cover the saucepan with a lid and leave to simmer-cook for 20–25 minutes. Now is the time to make the scones. The soup is cooked when the lentils are disintegrating. When it has reached this point, whizz until creamy smooth, adjust the seasoning and serve with your freshly made Cheese and Chive Scones.

Allium Soup

Feeds 6: The allium family covers leeks, onions, chives and garlic, all stuffed with health-giving properties, not to mention their taste-giving properties. And all are included in this delightful soup; soft, sweet and gentle, it can be eaten by anybody and enjoyed by all.

What you need: 2 knobs **butter**
2 tbsp **extra virgin olive oil**
2 **onions, peeled and sliced**
2 **leeks, roots cut off and chopped**
1 large **potato, peeled and chopped**
4 cloves **garlic, peeled and crushed**
6 cups/1.5 l **Veggie Stock (page 69)**
sea salt and freshly ground black pepper

1 tbsp **fresh chives, chopped**
1 tbsp **organic bio-live natural yoghurt**

Homemade Chips (page 45)
Cheese and Chive Scones (page 148)

What you do: Melt the butter in a saucepan on a medium heat. Add the chopped potatoes, onions, leeks, garlic and a good slosh of olive oil. Toss to ensure everything is well covered. Sauté with the lid on for 9–10 minutes, stirring occasionally to make sure that it doesn't burn. When all looks soft and golden, add the stock. Season generously. Bring to the boil then reduce the heat and simmer for 20–25 minutes. While the soup is cooking make your Chips or Cheese and Chive Scones. When everything is soft, remove the soup from the heat and blend until completely smooth. Serve piping hot with a dollop of yoghurt, a sprinkle of chives and the Chips or Cheese and Chive Scones.

Bacon and Cabbage Soup

Feeds 4: This is similar to an Italian recipe where a piece of beef is used to flavour a sauce then removed when the sauce is cooked. We take the bacon out before we whizz the soup. Bacon and Cabbage Soup is a new twist on that most maligned combination of Irish cooking; don't be put off, do try it. The bacon adds a gorgeous salty depth to an already tasty soup.

What you need: 1 tbsp **extra virgin olive oil**
2 **onions, peeled and chopped**
1 piece **organic bacon**
1 small **cabbage, sliced**
1 knob **butter**
2 cloves **garlic, peeled and crushed**
6 cups/1.5 l **Veggie Stock (page 69)**
1 tbsp **fresh parsley, chopped**
freshly ground black pepper

Homemade Chips (page 45)

What you do: Sauté the onion with the olive oil in a large saucepan on a low heat. When the onion has turned pale gold, put the piece of bacon on top and season generously with pepper (there's no need for salt as the bacon provides plenty). Cook for several minutes. Now add the cabbage and garlic, topped with a knob of butter. Stir to ensure everything is coated and cook for another few minutes. Then add the stock. Bring to the boil, then reduce and simmer for a further 12–15 minutes. If you are making Chips, now is the time to cook them. When the soup is cooked through, remove from the heat and take out the piece of bacon. Whizz the soup until smooth. Serve with a sprinkle of parsley and perhaps a portion of Homemade Chips.

Mulligatawny
(Spicy Chicken Soup)

Feeds 4: This is the most scrumptious chicken soup you'll ever find. From India (mulla ga tani – pepper water), it was a favourite with the British during the days of the Raj. And it is pepper water, hot and spicy, so don't devour the whole pot if you're very sensitive.

What you need:
1 tbsp **extra virgin olive oil**
1 **large onion, peeled and chopped**
4 cloves **garlic, peeled and crushed**
4 **cardamon pods**
4 **cloves**
1 **cinnamon stick**
4 **curry leaves**
12 **whole coriander seeds**
1 tbsp **ground coriander**
1 tsp **ground cumin**
1 tsp **turmeric**
2 good-sized **chicken breasts, sliced into 1 cm strips**
5 cups/1.25 l **Veggie Stock (page 69)**
sea salt and freshly ground black pepper

Chapati (page 150)
a bowl **organic bio-live yoghurt**

What you do: Gently fry the onion and garlic in the olive oil over a medium heat until soft and golden, say 6–8 minutes. Meanwhile prepare the chicken. Now add all the spices to the onion and garlic mixture. Mix well and cook for several minutes longer. Next, add the chicken pieces and stir again to coat the chicken in the spices. Cook for several more minutes, turning the chicken until browned on all sides. Season generously. The last thing to go in is the stock. Then cook on a simmering heat for 30–35 minutes. While the soup is cooking, make the Chapati. Once thoroughly cooked and smelling scrumptious, take off the heat, remove the cinnamon stick and liquidise, or serve chunky. Taste. Adjust seasoning. Serve with Chapati on the side and a bowl of natural yoghurt. Oh yeah …

Basic Chicken Stock

Makes approx. 1 litre: Chicken soup is definitely food for the soul – and body, and mind – but to get the chicken soup hit, you have to make the stock yourself. Just take the carcass of the chicken you and your loved ones have just devoured, plus any bones left over, put all into a saucepan with lots of nice vegetables (the same ones you would use for veggie stock). Bring to the boil and simmer for as long as possible (an hour is about the minimum, 2 to 3 hours is even better).

What you need:
1 **chicken carcass and bones**
2 **onions (with skin still on) chopped in half**
1 **leek, chopped in half**
1 **large carrot**
2–3 **outer leaves cabbage/2–3 winter/spring greens**
1 **stick celery/several leaves lovage**
2 **garlic cloves (with skin still on), chopped in half**
1 **bouquet garni (bay leaves/thyme/parsley/sage/ rosemary)**
1.5 l **water**

What you do: Put the chicken carcass in a large saucepan with a tight-fitting lid. Scrub the vegetables and remove any grotty bits. Put them all into the pan. Cover with cold water, bring to the boil and let simmer. Remove any scum that rises to the surface and allow to cool. Once cool, remove the fat from the surface, and *voilà*, your very own, delicious chicken stock which can be frozen for later use.

French Onion Soup

Feeds 4: French Onion Soup is a classic and this version from Bordeaux will have them begging for more. Onions are the most wonderful food; long valued in country medicine for helping to clear everything from colds to rheumatism. This soup rests entirely on the quality of the onions and the stock, so make sure you have the best possible. Organic onions can be bought in most supermarkets and they really are worth eating, unlike their non-organic counterparts. If you're sensitive to eggs, just leave the egg yolk out.

What you need: 2 tbsp **extra virgin olive oil**
4 large **onions, sliced**
2 cloves **garlic, peeled and crushed**
4 cups/1 l **Veggie Stock (page 69)**
1 **free-range egg yolk**
sea salt and freshly ground black pepper

Farls (page 146)
1 tbsp **chives, chopped**

What you do: Warm the olive oil on a medium heat. Then gently sauté the onions and garlic, with the saucepan lid on, until soft and transparent – be very careful not to let the onions burn. After 8–10 minutes add the stock. Season generously, cover again with the lid and simmer gently for 25–30 minutes. While the soup is cooking, make the Farls. When the time is up, remove the saucepan from the heat and liquidise. In a small bowl beat the egg yolk, then slowly add a ladleful of the soup to the egg; go slowly, as you don't want to curdle it. Now pour the egg mixture back into the soup, and mix gently. Warm slowly, not allowing to boil. Pour into 4 bowls, garnish with the chives and serve with a Farl.

Cockyleekie Soup

Feeds 4: 'Cockyleekie' (cock/hen cooked with leeks) is from Scotland, where they know a thing or two about keeping out winter wet and cold. We make this soup post-Roast Chicken when we have all the ingredients to hand – cold chicken and oodles of chicken stock – to make a delightful feast. The key to making this soup delicious is the stock: make your own.

What you need: 1 knob **butter**
1 tbsp **extra virgin olive oil**
2 **onions, peeled and sliced**
2 good-sized/4 small **leeks, roots cut off, washed and chopped**
1 cup **cooked chicken meat**
6 cups/1.5 l **Chicken Stock (page 76)**
sea salt and freshly ground black pepper

Farls (page 146)

What you do: Follow the usual soup-making steps: scrub, peel and chop all your veg and sauté in olive oil until golden and translucent. Add a knob of butter and season generously. Stir. Cook for further minute or so. Now add the stock. Bring to the boil, reduce the heat, cover and cook gently for 15–20 minutes. While the soup is cooking, make your Farls. It's up to you whether or not you want the soup liquidised or not. To liquidise, simply whizz until smooth. Taste. Adjust the seasoning if necessary.

Luke's Potato and Carrot Soup

Feeds 4: This is a wonderful winter soup, gentle on the digestion and delicious to boot.

What you need:
2 knobs **butter**
2 tbsp **extra virgin olive oil**
3 **onions, peeled and chopped**
6 **scallions, chopped**
4 cloves **garlic, peeled and crushed**
4 large **carrots, peeled and chopped**
1 large **potato, peeled and chopped**
6 cups/1.5 l **Veggie Stock (page 69)**
1 tbsp **fresh parsley**
sea salt and freshly ground black pepper

Homemade Chips (page 45)

What you do: On a medium heat, warm the olive oil. Add the scallions, garlic and onion. Sauté on a gentle to medium heat for 5 minutes, making sure they don't stick or burn. Now add the potato and carrot. Stir well, add one knob of butter and season generously. Next, add the stock and swirl in the second knob of butter. If you're making Chips, now is the time to put them on. Adjust the seasoning. Simmer gently for 15–20 minutes until all the veggies are really soft. Remove from the heat and blend. Serve at once with a dollop of yoghurt, a sprinkle of parsley and perhaps a Farl or Cheese and Chive Scone.

Libby's Sweet Soup

If after perfecting Luke's delicious Potato and Carrot Soup you fancy trying a variation, try replacing the **potato, peeled and chopped** with 1 large or 2 small **parsnips, peeled and chopped**, for a delicious, super-sweet soup. We need to say a big thank you to the superchef who provided this variation: thanks Libby!

Chickpea Soup with Lime Cream

Feeds 4: Like a lot of our soups, Chickpea Soup is heavenly comfort food, perfect when you need to eat simply. However, it can be happily dolled up to suit any occasion with the addition of the lime cream – it gives me a warm feeling just thinking about it! You'll notice this recipe is very similar to Blazing Salads Soup, with a few changes. And a confession: I nicked the idea of using a lime cream to pep up the soup from another of our favourite books, *The New Cranks Recipe Book* by Nadine Abensur. Thanks!

What you need:
2 tbsp extra **virgin olive oil**
3–4 cloves **garlic, peeled and crushed**
1 large **onion, peeled and chopped**
1 tin **cooked chickpeas, junk-free**
2 tsp each **ground cumin and coriander**
2 tsp **cayenne pepper**
1 tbsp **fresh rosemary and parsley, chopped**
5 cups/1.25 l **water** *or* **Veggie Stock (page 69)**
sea salt and freshly ground black pepper
2 tbsp **organic bio-live natural yoghurt**
1 **lime, juiced**
a pinch **cayenne pepper**

Cheese and Chive Scones (page 148)

What you do: Sauté the onion, garlic and olive oil in a saucepan on a medium heat for 7–8 minutes without allowing them to brown. Now add the chickpeas, spices, herbs and stock. Season generously, bring to the boil then reduce the heat. Cover the saucepan with a lid and leave to simmer-cook for 20–25 minutes. Now you can make your scones. Also, make the lime cream by mixing the yoghurt and lime juice. The soup is cooked when the chickpeas are disintegrating. When the soup has reached this point, whizz until creamy smooth. Adjust the seasoning, pour into 4 bowls, with a dollop of the lime cream on top and sprinkle with a little bit of cayenne pepper.

Pasta Dishes

There's something about pasta: without it life just isn't quite the same. Like bread, pasta is one of those things which pre-allergies will (probably) have been a major part of your yums. Post-allergies you will probably find it quite hard to find a pasta that's tasty. We've tried all the alternative varieties, but the only one we have found that tastes – and behaves – like normal pasta, is spelt; we now always eat spelt out of preference. If you are gluten intolerant use millet. So welcome back to the world of pasta! All our pasta dishes can be pulled together in under half an hour, making them the ultimate fast food – in fact just what fast food should be: quick, tasty, filling and nutritious.

Warm Pasta, Spicy Olive Oil and Salty Cheese Salad

Feeds 4: Although Luke would never dream of eating this recipe, he was the one who came up with it. This is a very simple dish – herbs, cheese, olive oil and spicy chilli with pasta. Serve with a Green Salad for a light meal.

What you need:
500 g **spelt *or* organic wheat pasta**
4 tbsp **extra virgin olive oil**
2 cloves **garlic, peeled and crushed**
4 **scallions, peeled and chopped**
½ tbsp **fresh rosemary, finely chopped**
1 tbsp **fresh basil, chopped**
4 chunks **organic cheese of your choice (we use feta)**
2 tbsp **Harissa (page 160)**
sea salt and freshly ground black pepper

What you do: Cook the pasta in a large pot of boiling water until al dente, so it retains some bite, about 10 minutes. Meanwhile, warm the olive oil in a heavy-bottomed saucepan. Add the garlic, scallions and herbs. Sauté for 3–4 minutes until it is all soft and golden, but not yet browning. Leave to one side while the pasta finishes cooking. When the pasta is cooked, drain it, return to the heat and toss with the sauce. Remove from the heat, crumble through the cheese, season generously and allow to marinate for a few minutes. Now add the Harissa, if you're using it. Serve on 4 plates, generously seasoned, with a drizzle of seasoned olive oil.

Zucchini Pasta

Feeds 2: Zucchini are in fact courgettes, but the name sounds so good in Italian. Having despised courgettes for years, we tried this recipe and now know what we were missing! Pay very close attention the first time you cook this recipe – the courgettes have a tendency to be happily cooking, and then wham they are ready and you need to get them off the heat quickly. The leftovers are also wonderful as a cold salad next day or as an evening snack.

What you need: 2 **courgettes, sliced into slim rounds**
2 tbsp **extra virgin olive oil**
250 g **spelt *or* organic wheat pasta**
3 **scallions, chopped**
1 large clove **garlic, peeled and chopped**
3 **tomatoes, chopped**
a piece **lemon**
1 tbsp **fresh parsley and basil, torn**
sea salt and freshly ground black pepper

What you do: Take a large frying pan, place on a medium heat and add half the olive oil. When the oil has warmed up, add the courgettes, a pinch of salt and lashings of black pepper. The courgette needs frequent stirring to prevent scorching. Once the courgette has been on for 7 minutes and is starting to soften, put the pasta on. The courgette is cooked after another 5 minutes or so, when it's starting to turn pale golden brown and looks caramelised. Now add the scallions, garlic and tomatoes. Season generously. Cook for a few minutes more or until the tomato is perfectly soft, then add the cooked pasta and the herbs. Squeeze the piece of lemon over it all. Serve at once or allow to cool and eat as a salad.

Spaghetti Bolognese

Feeds 4: Spaghetti Bolognese makes a good, filling meal, perfect for feeding empty people. It is also idiot proof, just cook it thoroughly. It is very simple for the times when you need to cook on auto pilot. If you are vegetarian or vegan, replace the organic mince with the same weight organic tofu, for an equally gorgeous Bolognese.

What you need:
2 tbsp **extra virgin olive oil**
3 cloves **garlic, peeled and crushed**
2 **onions, peeled and chopped**
250 g **organic minced beef**
1 tin **tomatoes, chopped**
½ tbsp **fresh basil, finely chopped**
sea salt and freshly ground black pepper
500 g **spelt *or* organic wheat pasta**

sprinkle of cheese (optional)

What you do: Sauté the onion and garlic in the olive oil for 5–6 minutes until the onion becomes soft and transparent. Add the mince and mix around to coat in the oil. Cook on a medium heat for a further 4–5 minutes or until the mince is lightly browned. Chuck in the tomatoes, basil and a further slosh of olive oil. Season generously. Mix it all together and leave to simmer for about 20 minutes. After the sauce has been on for 15 minutes, start the pasta. Cook the pasta in a saucepan full of boiling water on a simmering heat. The pasta and sauce will both finish cooking at around the same time; use your judgement, but the pasta will take about 8–10 minutes. Strain the pasta and serve immediately with the sauce on top, perhaps with a drizzle of olive oil and a sprinkle of cheese.

Spicy Spaghetti Bolognese

We love Spaghetti Bolognese as it is but Luke disagrees; apparently it is too wimpy! If, like Luke, you prefer your food to bite back, try adding ½ tsp **chilli *or* cayenne powder**, ½ tsp **ground cumin** and ½ tsp **ground coriander** to the above recipe when you add the mince.

Bacon Sauce with Pasta

Feeds 4: Bacon sauce is for those who cannot resist having some form of meat in everything they eat. This dish is a hot and spicy tummy warmer.

What you need:
2 tbsp **extra virgin olive oil**
4–5 **scallions, chopped**
4 **rashers of bacon, cut into strips**
1 large **tomato, roughly chopped**
3 cloves **garlic, peeled and crushed**
1 onion, peeled and chopped
1 tin **tomatoes, chopped**
6–8 **leaves fresh basil**
2 tsp **chilli powder**
1 tsp **ground turmeric**
sea salt and freshly ground black pepper
400 g **spelt** or **organic wheat pasta**

a sprinkle of **cheese**

What you do: Put a pan onto a warm heat and add a slosh of olive oil to the bottom of the pan. Throw in the bacon. Stir. Season generously. After 2–3 minutes, add the garlic, scallions and onion. Cook for 5–6 more minutes on a medium heat. Then add the tinned tomatoes, tomato, basil, chilli powder and ground turmeric. Stir. Put the lid on the pan and leave to cook for 10 minutes. While the sauce cooks, put the pasta on. Bring a pan of water to the boil, add the pasta and cook for 10 minutes. Strain the pasta and take the sauce off the heat. Put the pasta on a plate and add the sauce. Season well and serve at once with a sprinkle of cheese.

Spaghetti alla Carbonara

Feeds 4: You know those days when you absolutely must have something cream-laden? So here we present a Green Spaghetti alla Carbonara. As with a lot of our recipes, this is a classic dish Green-ified, with a gorgeous, creamy sauce and salty bacon strips. Serve with a Green Salad to cut through the creamy pasta. Or not ...

What you need: 500 g **spelt or organic wheat pasta**
5 **rashers streaky bacon**
2 **free-range egg yolks**
½ cup/125 ml **extra virgin olive oil**
½ cup/125 ml **organic bio-live natural yoghurt**
2 cloves **garlic, peeled and crushed**
½ cup **organic cheddar cheese, or feta**
1 tbsp **fresh basil and parsley, finely chopped**
sea salt and freshly ground black pepper

What you do: Cook the pasta in a large saucepan with lots of boiling water and a pinch of salt. As the pasta will take about 10 minutes on a medium heat, you have plenty of time to prepare the sauce. Start by frying the bacon with a dash of olive oil for 5–6 minutes or until golden brown. Meanwhile make the saucy part – a version of mayonnaise. Start by adding a drop of olive oil to the egg yolk, gently mixing it into the yolk with a small whisk. Add the second drop, then mix in again. Always make sure to combine the last drop of oil before adding the next. Slowly increase the amount of oil, but be careful or the mixture will curdle. Once the egg has absorbed all the oil, leave to one side while you get the pasta. When the pasta is cooked, drain it, then return to the saucepan. Add a slosh of olive oil and 'dry-out' most of the wet, for about 30 seconds. Turn off the heat. Add the mayo to the pasta and stir to coat the pasta. Whatever you do, don't turn your back on the heat, you don't want scrambled eggs! Now, cut the bacon into thin strips and add the yoghurt, parsley, cooked bacon and 2 cloves of peeled, crushed garlic. Stir again and season generously. Serve at once, with a Green Salad.

Green Basil Pesto with Pasta

Feeds 4: Pesto from jars is so vile it's worth making your own just to see what it should taste like. Pasta with Pesto is a classic combination, a simple, sophisticated dinner that will take 10 minutes to prepare. Or if you happen to have a jar of our wonderful Pesto (page 161) pre-made, then this will take only as long as the pasta needs to cook. To save time, you don't have to toast the pine nuts, though considering it's going to take the pasta a bit of time to cook, you might as well.

What you need:
1 cup **pine nuts**
3 tbsp **extra virgin olive oil**
a squeeze **fresh lemon juice**
1–2 cloves **garlic, peeled and crushed**
2–4 handfuls **fresh basil**
1 large lump **feta cheese**
sea salt and freshly ground black pepper
500 g **spelt** *or* **organic wheat pasta**

What you do: Preheat the oven to 230°C/450°F/gas mark 8. Spread the pine nuts out on a baking sheet and pop into the oven for 10–15 minutes or until they are golden brown. Meanwhile, cook the pasta in a large pot of boiling water until it's al dente, say 8–10 minutes. Continue with the pesto. You have a choice for making the pesto: a blender, or a mortar and pestle. If using a pestle and mortar, chop up the basil then chuck in and crush all the ingredients in your mortar. If using a blender, whizz all the ingredients together. The consistency is up to you – we prefer to use a pestle and mortar, as you get a rougher, chunkier pesto, but some people prefer a smoother, more shop-bought consistency. Try both, see what you prefer. When the pasta is cooked, mix the pasta, pesto and cheese in a large serving bowl. Season generously. Serve at once.

Spelt Pasta with Broad Beans, Tomatoes and Goat's Cheese

Feeds 4: If you have ever read Sophie Grigson's *Organics*, a truly wonderful cookbook, you might be surprised by how similar this recipe is to one of hers. Purely accidental! Chupi was starving one day and spotted broad beans, goat's cheese, sun-dried tomatoes and pasta in the kitchen. She made this dish by flinging them together. Months later she was shocked to discover an almost identical recipe in *Organics*. Thus, this gorgeous, quick, tasty recipe had better be dedicated to Sophie Grigson.

What you need:
400 g **shelled broad beans**
2 tbsp **extra virgin olive oil**
2 cloves **garlic, peeled and crushed**
about 20–25 **Sun-Dried Tomatoes (page 41)**
¼–½ cup **organic soft goat's cheese**
1 tbsp each **fresh basil and parsley, finely chopped**
sea salt and freshly ground black pepper
500 g **spelt *or* organic wheat pasta**

What you do: Put a large pan of water on to boil and when the water is boiling, add the pasta. Leave to cook for 8–10 minutes until al dente. Meanwhile, warm the olive oil on a medium heat. Add the beans. Cook gently, stirring occasionally, for about 5–6 minutes. Add the tomatoes and garlic. Cook for a further minute then remove from the heat until the pasta is ready. When the pasta is cooked, drain and return to the pan. Add the bean mixture, cheese and herbs. Warm up on a gentle heat. Serve with a Green Salad.

Classic Tomato and Basil Sauce with Pasta

Feeds 4: This uncomplicated and tasty meal can be pulled together in minutes. Everyone loves pasta with a Classic Tomato Sauce, but it's very hard to find a decent version of it. A lot of people just use sauce out of a jar. You might as well use tomato ketchup – unhealthy and vile. Proper tomato sauce is so simple, it's worth making your own. Many cooks believe you should add sugar to all tomato dishes, but there's no need; tomatoes are very sweet, they just have to be cooked properly. This is perfect summer fodder, served with a Green Salad and perhaps a nice bottle of booze if allowed!

What you need:
2 tbsp **extra virgin olive oil**
2 cloves **garlic, peeled and crushed**
1 large **onion, peeled and chopped**
2 tins **tomatoes, chopped**
1 cup **tomato passata**
1 tbsp **fresh basil**
sea salt and freshly ground black pepper
500 g **spelt or organic wheat pasta**
sprinkle of **cheese**

What you do: Warm the olive oil in a heavy-bottomed saucepan. Add the onion and garlic and sauté for 5–6 minutes. Add the tomatoes, tomato passata and basil. Season generously and leave to cook for a further 15–20 minutes. The pasta should go on 10 minutes before you expect the sauce to be cooked. Cook the pasta in a large pot of boiling water until al dente. When both the pasta and sauce are cooked, drain the pasta, return to the pan and allow to dry out for about 30 seconds. Chuck in the tomato sauce, toss together and serve at once on 4 plates with a sprinkle of cheese and a drizzle of olive oil.

Veggie Meals

There are those who believe that unless there's something dead and roasted in the middle of the table it isn't a meal, though luckily there are lots of the other kind of people as well. This chapter is for them and, while they're scoffing their way through their delicious meal, let them pretend not to notice the hand creeping in from the side, 'Do you mind if I just try a mouthful?' Yes, Veggie Meals are for everyone, even if you have to compromise and pretend there's something dead in the meal! And if you are one of those 'if it's not dead it's not edible' types, then please give us an opportunity to convert you, if not to a strictly vegetarian way of eating, to at least the occasional enjoyment of a gorgeous veggie meal.

Piperade

Feeds 4: Apparently in France this tasty dish is served as breakfast. Well, it would make a very tasty brekkie, but you'd need a clear space in which to cook it; try Sunday morning, the perfect day on which to enjoy a large brunch and the newspapers.

What you need: 2 tbsp **extra virgin olive oil**
2 cloves **garlic, peeled and crushed**
1 large **onion, peeled and chopped**
5 **tomatoes, chopped**
1 **red pepper, deseeded and cut into .5 cm strips**
4 **free-range eggs**
sea salt and freshly ground black pepper

4 **Farls (page 146)**

What you do: Warm the olive oil in a heavy-bottomed frying pan. Add the onion and garlic and sauté for 5 minutes on a medium heat. Now add the peppers. Season generously and cook for a further 5 minutes. Then add the tomatoes to the pan and cook for another 10 minutes. Make the Farls while the stew continues cooking. When the sauce is ready, make 4 hollows in it and into each hollow break an egg. Cook for 4–5 minutes more or until the eggs are cooked to your liking. Serve each egg with a quarter of the Piperade and a Farl.

The Ultimate Veggie Burger and Chips

Feeds 4: For years we tried to make a veggie burger that a) tastes nice; and b) didn't disintegrate on contact with heat. Success at last! We absolutely adore these burgers. A note of advice: you must use all the toppings to get the Ultimate hit. On the subject of bread, we find Farls to be so perfect and so easy we always use them. However, if you want to replace them with suitable 'Green' bread, do.

The Burgers

What you need:
1 tsp each **ground cumin and coriander**
1 tbsp **fresh parsley, chopped**
1 cup/110 g **gram flour**
1 tin **cooked chickpeas, drained and whizzed**
4 **scallions, chopped**
4 cloves **garlic, peeled and crushed**
3 tsp **lemon juice, freshly squeezed**
1 tbsp **extra virgin olive oil**
sea salt and freshly ground black pepper

The Buns

What you need:
3 cups/450 g **white spelt** *or* **organic wheat flour**
1 tsp **bread soda**
¾ cup/188 ml **water** *or* **rice, oat, soya** *or* **cow's milk**
1 tbsp **bio-live natural yoghurt**

The Extras

What you need:
8 slices **organic feta cheese**
2 **tomatoes, very thinly sliced**
salad leaves
¼ **red onion, very thinly sliced**
2 tbsp **Mayonnaise (page 159)**
Harissa (page 160)
sea salt and freshly ground pepper

Homemade Chips (page 45)

What you do: Get your burgers together first. Whizz the chickpeas to a lumpy consistency. Add the rest of the burger ingredients and combine with a spoon – if it's too sticky, add more gram flour. Season generously. There should be enough mix for about 8 burgers – just store whatever you don't need in the fridge. Dust your hands with plenty of flour, take 4 handfuls of mix, roll each into a ball then flatten into burgers about 1 cm thick. Now you can get the chips on. Warm half a tablespoon of olive oil in a large frying pan. Add the 4 burgers and cook on a medium heat for 4–5 minutes per side or until done to your liking. While the burgers are cooking, make the buns. Mix all the bun ingredients together, to form a soft, not too sticky dough. Divide into 4 balls and flatten to 1 cm thick. Put another frying pan on a medium heat and sprinkle with flour. When the flour starts to brown, put the Buns on for about 4 minutes per side. To serve, slice the Buns in half, plonk on the burger, add a couple of slices of cheese, a twist of pepper and salt, a few salad leaves, the red onion, the tomato, some Garlic Mayonnaise and some Harissa. Serve with Pomme Frites or plain ol' Chips and a Green Salad.

The Green Margarita

Feeds 4: Pizza is our universal favourite meal. However, most 'normal' pizza is poison with the base made from commercial wheat and yeast, the sauce a suspicious tomato and sugar goo. As for the topping? Don't even go there! We've tried numerous recipes to come up with the perfect pizza: a crisp, chewy base, a sweet tomato sauce and delicious cheese topping. This is definitely the work of 4 people. We proudly present the Green Margarita. This makes 2 pizzas – in our opinion just enough for 4 people.

The Sauce
What you need:
2 tbsp **extra virgin olive oil**
3 cloves **garlic, peeled and crushed**
2 **scallions, peeled and chopped**
1 **onion, peeled and chopped**
1 tin **tomatoes, chopped**
1 cup **tomato passata**
1 tbsp **fresh basil, torn**
few sprigs **rosemary, finely chopped**
sea salt and freshly ground black pepper

The Base
What you need:
3 cups/450 g **white spelt** or **organic wheat flour**
1 tsp **bread soda**
1 tsp **dried thyme**
¾ cup/188 ml **water** or **rice, oat, soya or cow's milk**

The Topping
What you need:
your favourite cheese (we use **feta, chopped**)
6 **tomatoes, thinly sliced**
1 tbsp **fresh basil, torn**
few sprigs **rosemary, chopped**
1 tbsp **extra virgin olive oil**
sea salt and freshly ground black pepper

What you do: Start with the sauce. Sauté the onion, garlic and scallions in the olive oil for 5–7 minutes until soft on a medium heat. While that's cooking, start the base, using the basic Farl recipe from page 146. Get a mixing bowl, mix the dry ingredients and make a well in the centre. Add the liquid and mix until all the liquid is absorbed. You should have a soft, not too sticky, dough. Give it another knead, then form it into a ball, divide in half and roll each out into a circle no more than .75 cm thick. Get out a large frying pan, put on a medium heat and sprinkle with flour. Back to the sauce. Add the tomato, passata and herbs to the onions and garlic. Season well and leave to cook while you continue with the base. When the flour starts to brown, lift the base on to the pan, with the aid of a wooden spoon. Cook each base for 3–7 minutes per side until lightly browned. By the time this is done, the sauce should be perfect. Put the bases on 2 circular baking tins. Slather the sauce on top and sprinkle with the cheese. Layer on the slices of tomato, scatter the herbs, season generously and slosh over the olive oil. Pop under the grill for about 10 minutes or until the cheese has melted. While the pizzas are finishing, make the Green Salad. Serve at once.

Chilli Without Carne

Feeds 4: Chilli without meat? Strange as it may sound some prefer chilli without carne – we use organic tofu instead as it's so good. Of course if you must, you can substitute organic minced beef, but I can't really see the point as the end result is very similar and it does everyone good to eat veggie occasionally. We've all tried chilli so there is no need to enumerate the benefits of this hot, tasty dish. There aren't any secrets, except to be careful when you're cooking the tofu as you don't want it to completely disintegrate.

What you need: 2 **onions, finely chopped**
4 cloves **garlic, peeled and crushed**
1 tbsp **extra virgin olive oil**
1 block **organic tofu, cut into 1 cm cubes**
1 tin **tomatoes, chopped**
½ tin **kidney beans, rinsed**
3 tsp each **ground cumin, coriander and dried chilli powder**
1 tbsp **fresh parsley, basil and rosemary, chopped**
sea salt and freshly ground black pepper

3½ cups/875 ml **water**
1½ cups **basmati rice**

1 quantity **Nachos (page 51)** *or*
1 quantity **Tortillas (page 144)**
dollop **organic bio-live natural yoghurt**

What you do: Sauté the onion and garlic in the olive oil for 4–5 minutes or until translucent. Now add the tofu and stir gently to ensure that it is evenly coated in the olive oil. Allow to cook for a further 5–6 minutes until the tofu is lightly browned. Then add the tomatoes, beans, spices and herbs. Season generously. Bring the chilli up to a simmer, then reduce the heat, put a lid on the saucepan and leave to cook for 30–40 minutes on a medium heat. Meanwhile, prepare the Nachos or Tortillas, whichever you have chosen. Ten minutes before the chilli is cooked, put the basmati rice and water into a saucepan with a tight lid. Cook the rice on a medium heat. The rice and the chilli will be done around the same time, but keep an eye on both towards the end of their cooking time. Serve the chilli on the basmati with a dollop of yoghurt and the pile of Nachos or Tortillas for the ultimate Latin American inspired feast.

Peruvian Steak (page 114)

Spiced Chicken Wraps, delicious and delectable (page 121)

Luke going heavy on the Chilli Chicken Dippers (page 124)

We were going to do before and after pictures, but that would have been too depressing!

Chupi eating Brian's Spicy Chicken Curry with Organic Brown Rice (page 116). Ah, isn't love beautiful!

Fish Stew (page 105)

Chapati, a national treasure from India (page 150)

Mum's Spanish Omelette

Feeds 4: With its scrumptious, fortifying innards, Spanish Omelette really is eating and drinking. Make sure to get the best eggs you can and that all your ingredients are squeaky-clean fresh. A wonderful dish at any time of the night or day.

What you need:
1 tbsp **extra virgin olive oil**
4 **scallions, chopped**
2 cloves **garlic, peeled and crushed**
2 **very ripe tomatoes, chopped into chunks**
4 **cold cooked potatoes, chopped into rough 1 cm cubes**
1 tbsp **basil, rosemary and parsley, finely chopped**
4 **free-range eggs**
sea salt and freshly ground black pepper
2 **rashers of bacon, cut into strips** (optional)

4 **Farls (page 146)**

What you do: Place a large frying pan on a medium heat with a slosh of olive oil. If using the bacon, put into the pan while you prepare the rest of the ingredients. When the bacon is nearly cooked, add the scallions, garlic, tomatoes, cooked potato, herbs and remainder of the oil. Season with a little salt and generous amounts of pepper. Cook on a medium heat, stirring occasionally, for about 8–10 minutes. While the omelette mix is cooking, make the Farls. Break the eggs into a bowl, season and mix together. Remove the bacon and potato mixture onto a plate. Put the egg mixture into the hot frying pan. Swirl so that the mix covers the base of the frying pan and cook until it's just beginning to set, about 3 minutes. Spread the potato mix evenly over the omelette and allow to cook for a further 2–3 minutes. Slide the omelette off the pan, divide into 4 and serve each atop a toasted, halved Farl.

Kitchiri with Chapati

Feeds 4: Dhal from India is one of life's treats. This is the real thing, a genuine Indian Dhal served with genuine Indian Chapati. OK, not really, but this is damn close to the real thing.

What you need:
1 cup/200 g **green lentils**
2 tbsp **extra virgin olive oil**
1 knob **butter**
1 large **onion, peeled and finely chopped**
2 cloves **garlic, peeled and crushed**
1½ cups/300 g **basmati rice**
1 tsp **ground turmeric**
1 tsp each **black mustard, cumin, cardamom and fennel seeds**
3 tsp each **ground cumin and coriander**
3 **bay leaves**
4 **cloves**
1 **cinnamon stick**
4 cups/1 l **water** *or* **vegetable stock**
1 cup **passata** *or* **chopped tinned tomatoes**
1 tbsp **fresh parsley, chopped**
sea salt and freshly ground black pepper

1 quantity **Chapati (page 150)**
a bowl **organic bio-live natural yoghurt**

What you do: Soak the lentils in enough boiling water to cover them while you prepare the rest of the ingredients. Put the butter, olive oil, chopped onion and crushed garlic into a large saucepan. Sauté gently on a medium heat for 5 minutes. Then add the basmati, herbs and spices, mix well, and cook for a few minutes more. When that's done, add the lentils, stock and tomatoes and season generously. Bring to the boil, put a lid on the saucepan then reduce the heat. Cover and simmer for half an hour or until all the stock is absorbed and the lentils and rice are soft but still retaining some 'bite'. If you're making the Chapati, now's the time to do it. When the dahl is cooked, adjust the seasoning to your taste and add the parsley. Serve with the Chapati, a bowl of natural yoghurt and perhaps a Green Salad.

Cianfotta
(Mediterranean Vegetable Stew)

Feeds 4: Chupi was once so sensitive that the idea of eating sweet peppers made her shudder, but thanks to good food and good work on the health front, she can now enjoy this beautiful combination of sweet Mediterranean vegetables. It's very easy to prepare, as it can be left to stew while you make a myriad of accompaniments. Cianfotta is gorgeous as a vegetable dish or as a main meal with a chunk of bread or some brown rice. As a bonus, it can be eaten cold the next day. Delish. We've also included a recipe variation for Ratatouille.

What you need:
3 tbsp **extra virgin olive oil**
1 **onion, peeled and chopped**
6 cloves **garlic, peeled and halved**
6 large **very ripe tomatoes, chopped into chunks**
1 **red pepper, deseeded and cut into 1 cm strips**
1 **yellow pepper, deseeded and cut into 1 cm strips**
1 medium **courgette, chopped into circles .5 cm thick**
1 handful **fresh basil leaves**
sea salt and freshly ground black pepper

4–5 cups/875 ml **water**
2 cups/400 g **shortgrain brown rice**

4 **Farls (page 146)**

What you do: Sauté the onion in half the olive oil until tender. Add the remaining vegetables. Stir to ensure all the veggies are evenly coated with the olive oil. Season generously. Cook on a low heat with the saucepan lid on for 40–45 minutes until the vegetables are soft but not disintegrating. While the stew is cooking, make the Farls. Put the rice on when the stew has been cooking for roughly 25 minutes. Put the rice and 4–5 cups of water in a saucepan with a tight-fitting lid on a medium heat (it should be cooked at the same time as the stew). Serve the stew on the bed of rice, perhaps with the Farls.

Ratatouille

Cianfotta is the Italian version of that much more famous vegetable stew, Ratatouille. However, for our version of Cianfotta, we don't include aubergine. If you feel like trying a Ratatouille, simply add 1 **aubergine, diced**, at the same time as the rest of the vegetables. Also, if you want to spice it up and remain true to the original, add 1 tsp **paprika** at the same time as the aubergine. Ta-da! Your Cianfotta is now a Ratatouille.

Winter Roast Roots

Feeds 4: An excellent middle-of-winter dish, the roasting caramelises the veggies to sweet perfection. We'd normally eat this as an evening meal with a Green Salad for contrast, and lots of dips, say Harissa, Aioli and Hummus. Vary your choice according to your taste. One question about this recipe is whether or not to peel the vegetables: it's a matter of personal choice, but we generally peel all those that aren't organic and just scrub those that are.

What you need: 6 **potatoes, scrubbed, halved if small, quartered if large**
4 **carrots, cut in half lengthways**
2 **onions, not peeled, quartered**
2 **parsnips, cut in half lengthways**
2–3 **baby turnips**
2 **beetroots, halved**
any other root vegetables in season
8–10 cloves **garlic, not peeled, whole**
few sprigs **rosemary**
few **bay leaves**
3 tbsp **extra virgin olive oil**
sea salt and freshly ground black pepper

Green Salad (page 61)

Harissa (page 160)
Aioli (page 159)
Hummus (page 56)

What you do: Preheat the oven to 200°C/400°F/gas mark 6. Put the prepared vegetables into a large roasting tray. Stuff the herbs in around them and over them. Drizzle with the olive oil, season with a lots of pepper and a few pinches of salt. Pop into the oven for 45 minutes, turning the veg halfway through the cooking time. While the vegetables are cooking, prepare the Green Salad, Harissa, Aioli and Hummus. Serve with a few chunks of feta mixed through, the Green Salad on the side and the dips in little bowls.

Courgette and Basmati Tart

Feeds 4: Real men, they say, don't eat quiche. Given the hideous and ubiquitous soggy confection universally on sale as quiche, it's surprising anyone does. But banish all thoughts of that quiche from your mind, this little baby, with its sweet crunchy pastry, delicious ingredients and intense texture will have real people, male and female, begging for more.

What you need:

1 cup/150 g **white spelt flour**
1 large knob **organic butter**
2 tbsp **extra virgin olive oil**
1 **free-range egg, beaten**
3 **shallots**
2 cloves **garlic**
2 tbsp **extra virgin olive oil**

2–3 **courgettes, sliced**
1 cup **basmati rice, cooked**
2 **free-range eggs, beaten**
2 chunks **organic cheese**
3–4 tbsp **organic bio-live natural yoghurt**
few sprigs **rosemary, chopped**
sea salt and freshly ground black pepper

Green Salad (page 61)
2 chunks **organic feta cheese** or a dollop **organic bio-live yoghurt**

What you do: Preheat your oven to 180°C/350°F/gas mark 4. To make the pastry: put the flour into a mixing bowl and rub in the butter until you have a crumbly, breadcrumb texture. Make a well in the centre and pour in the olive oil, egg and a splash of cold water if needed. Stir the flour into the liquid, mixing gently until you have a soft dough. Knead for 2–3 minutes. Put the dough in the fridge to rest. After about 20 minutes, take the pastry out of the fridge, oil a 20 cm deep tart tin and roll the pastry out to fit it. Prick the pastry all over with a fork and pop back into the fridge for another 5 minutes. Line the pastry case with greaseproof paper, weighed down with baking beans (any dry beans from your cupboard will do, provided you don't try to eat them afterwards!). Put the pastry case in the oven for 20 minutes. Meanwhile, prepare the filling. Sauté the shallots and garlic in the olive oil until soft, around 5–6 minutes. Then add the courgette. Stir and cook for a further 15 minutes on a gentle heat with the saucepan lid on. The pastry case will be ready a minute or so before the filling, so remove it from the oven. Remove the baking beans and paper and return to the oven for a further 4–5 minutes to crisp. While the pastry is completing its cooking, prepare the filling. Remove the courgette mix from the heat – it should be nicely cooked by now, soft and sweet. Mash roughly with a fork and allow to cool. Add the remaining ingredients and mix well. Season generously. Take the pastry case out of the oven. Pile the filling into the case, smooth down and drizzle over with olive oil. Bake in the oven for 30–35 minutes until golden. When the tart is almost cooked, make the Green Salad. Serve with a crumbling of cheese or a dollop of yoghurt and the Green Salad. Heaven.

Perfect Sautéed Rice

Feeds 4: Without a doubt, in times of hunger, this has been our culinary saviour, so simple, healing and tasty. I wouldn't touch the average fried rice, with its raw, crunchy ingredients and rubbery egg, but this is a delight: sweet tasty vegetables and rice. As with all recipes, experiment – if you're vegetarian, leave out the bacon; if you're a bamboo shoot nut, add them; if you dislike green beans, substitute broccoli. Just ensure that all your ingredients are tasty and fresh. Fried rice isn't meant to be all the leftovers in the fridge with rice. We've left the egg optional, as we prefer a gentler rice, but do add it if you want something more robust.

What you need: 2 tbsp **extra virgin olive oil**
3 **scallions, chopped**
2 cloves **garlic, peeled and crushed**
1 **rasher, cut into small slivers (optional)**
2 **very ripe tomatoes, chopped into chunks**
1 **small courgette, sliced and each slice halved**
1 handful **green beans, chopped into 1–2 cm bits** *or*
1 handful **broccoli, cut into florets**
4 cups **cooked shortgrain brown rice**
sea salt and freshly ground black pepper

1 **free-range egg (optional)**

2 chunks **organic feta cheese**

What you do: Place a large frying pan on a medium heat with a slosh of olive oil. If using bacon, put it into the pan while you prepare the rest of the ingredients. When the bacon is nearly cooked, add the scallions, garlic, tomatoes, and green beans (or broccoli). Season with a little salt and lots of black pepper. Find a large saucepan lid that neatly covers the pan – this prevents all the tasty juices evaporating. Cook on a medium heat, stirring occasionally, for about 8 minutes until everything is soft. Take the pan off the heat. Add the rice and mix together. Then, if you're using an egg, break it into the middle of the rice and mix thoroughly. Put the rice back on the heat and cook for a further 2–3 minutes until the egg is done to your liking; if not, just serve at once. Serve with some feta cheese crumbled through, drizzled with olive oil and a fresh Green Salad. Our favourite 'fast-food' meal.

Green Gratin Dauphinoise

Feeds 4: Slowly, slowly cooked gratin – layer upon layer of potatoes and onions baked in the oven – is a wonderful winter dish. For sensitive tums, it doesn't have to be cooked in litres of cream; substitute oatmilk, a creamy alternative to dairy milk, and best quality Veggie Stock.

What you need:
1 knob **butter**
1 tbsp **extra virgin olive oil**
8 large **potatoes, peeled and thinly sliced**
1 large **onion, peeled and thinly sliced**
3 cloves **garlic, peeled and crushed**
3 **scallions, chopped**
8 sprigs **rosemary, finely chopped**
2 cups/500 ml **oat milk**
2 cups/500 ml **Veggie Stock**
sea salt and freshly ground black pepper

Green Salad (page 61)
crumbled feta cheese

What you do: Preheat the oven to 170°C/325°F/gas mark 3. Grease an ovenproof gratin dish generously with oil and butter. Build up layers of potatoes, onions, garlic, sliced scallions, seasoning with salt and freshly ground black pepper and scattering with rosemary spears. Halfway up your gratin dish, pour in a mixture of oatmilk and stock up to the level of the potatoes. Then finish off the layers of vegetables. Pour in the remaining mixture of oatmilk and stock. Bake in the oven uncovered for 1½ hours until soft through and through. While the gratin is cooking, make the salad. When the gratin is cooked, crumble the feta over the top and serve with the Green Salad. And remember, gratin is, if anything, even more delicious re-heated the next day.

Fish Meals

When it comes to fish eating, all we can do is hold up our hands and say, guilty: our fish eating is still minimal. For the next book we plan to take up an invitation from a long-ago friend who has promised that if we come to an Atlantic hideaway, armed with skillet and knife, he will teach us everything there is to know of the glory of cooking and eating fish. That said, Luke's fish stew is absolutely delicious and can be adapted to almost any fish available. His pan-fried fish can also be adapted, so please forgive and, of what we do suggest, enjoy!

Fish Stew

Feeds 4: This stew is very good to eat for two reasons: it is very nutritious, and it tastes so very good!

What you need:
2 tbsp **extra virgin olive oil**
2 **onions, peeled and chopped**
4 **scallions, sliced**
1½ **cups shrimp, whole**
1 large **cod fillet, cut into cubes**
4 cloves **garlic, peeled and whole**
2 tins **chopped tomatoes**
½ tsp **chilli**
sea salt and freshly ground black pepper

What you do: Put a saucepan on a low heat. Sauté the onions slowly. Add the scallions and the garlic and cook, still nice and slow, for 10 minutes, until the onions, garlic and scallions are all soft and golden. Add the cod and the shrimp. Sauté for a further few minutes, turning gently so as not to break up the fish. Taste and then season. Add the tomatoes and the chilli. Taste again, put on a lid and stew, still nice and gently, for 30 minutes. Serve with organic basmati rice and a Green Salad.

Fried Fish

Feeds 4: This recipe is dedicated to our local chipper, as they still do chips as the universe intended. You can use fresh fillets of cod, haddock or plaice. We usually use haddock, but the choice is yours.

What you need: 2 tbsp **extra virgin olive oil**
4 fresh **fish fillets**
1 large **egg**
1½ cups/225g **white spelt** *or* **organic wheat flour**
1½ cups/375 ml **water**
4 slices **lemon**
sea salt and freshly ground black pepper

Homemade Chips (page 45)

What you do: Sieve the flour into a bowl. Add the olive oil and the water. Whisk to prevent lumps. Gently fold in the egg and leave for half an hour. Dip the fish fillets in the batter, making sure that the fillets are covered all over. When your fish is ready to go, start your chips. Now put the fish in the hot oil and cook for 10–15 minutes or until golden brown. Take them out with a slotted spoon and dry with kitchen paper. If there is any batter left, slice some onion into rings, dip in the batter and cook in the chip pan until brown – around 10 minutes. Serve the fish with a squeeze of lemon or if you can tolerate it, a little vinegar, and a heaped bowl of Homemade Chips.

Meat Meals

Let's face it, most men believe that there's no substitute for red meat and Luke believes this passionately too! But increasingly we are being told that with our relatively recent sedentary lifestyle, too much red meat is a bad thing. So keep full-on red-meat eating down. Make sure every bite is 100 per cent delicious, and 100 per cent additive free, by trying to buy organic. The taste difference is worth it and the health difference could be a life and death one.

The Classic Burger with Extras

Feeds 4: There's something so tasty about a burger in a soft chewy bun with fresh toppings, no wonder it's so many meat-lovers' favourite meal. It's easy to buy ready-made burgers, but if you've ever read the list of ingredients on one of the packets, you'll understand why it's important – considering it's so simple – to make your own. And do use all the extras for true enjoyment.

The Burger

What you need: 3 scallions, finely chopped
400 g organic minced beef
1 free-range egg yolk
2 cloves garlic, peeled and crushed
sea salt and freshly ground black pepper

The Buns

What you need: 3 cups/450 g white spelt *or* organic wheat flour
1 tsp bread soda
¾ cup/188 ml water *or* rice, oat, soya *or* cow's milk

The Extras

What you need: 2 tbsp Harissa (page 160)
8 slices organic cheese
salad leaves
2 tbsp Mayonnaise (page 159)

Homemade Chips (page 45)

What you do: If you're making Chips, get them on first, as you can keep them warm. Mix all the burger ingredients together and season generously. Split the mix into 4 pieces, roll into balls, then flatten into burgers about 2 cm thick. Warm half a tbsp of olive oil in a large frying pan. Add the 4 burgers and cook on a medium heat for 5–6 minutes each side or until done to your liking. If you are making Buns, mix all the ingredients together to form a soft dough. Divide into 4 balls, and flatten to 1 cm thick. Put another frying pan on a medium heat and sprinkle with flour. When the flour starts to brown, put the Buns on for about 4 minutes per side or until puffed up. To assemble, slice the Buns in half, spread each half with Harissa, plonk on the burger, add a couple of slices of cheese, a twist of pepper and salt, a few salad leaves, and some Aioli (page 159). Serve with Homemade Chips.

Spicy Meatballs in Tomato Sauce

Feeds 4: Meatballs do take a little time to prepare, but they are truly worth it. The spices make this one of the most heart- and tummy-warming dishes you could imagine. If you've gone off meat, find a good organic butcher – you can even get them online these days. Yes, it is more expensive, but just buy a little at a time and savour the difference. If you can't take meat in any shape or form, substitute red lentils or organic tofu, both available of which are in health food shops. Cook the meatballs carefully, as you don't want them to crumble.

The Meatballs

What you need: 400 g **organic minced beef**
1 **free-range egg yolk**
2 tsp each **ground turmeric and ground chilli**
2 cloves **garlic, peeled and crushed**
sea salt and freshly ground black pepper

The Sauce

What you need: 2 tbsp **extra virgin olive oil**
3 cloves **garlic, peeled and crushed**
2 **onions, peeled and chopped**
1 tin **tomatoes, chopped**
1 cup **tomato passata**
2 tsp each **ground cumin, turmeric and coriander**
2 tsp **ground chilli**
1 cup **organic bio-live natural yoghurt**
sea salt and freshly ground black pepper

2 cups/400 g **basmati rice**
4 cups/1 l **water**

Chapati (optional)

What you do: For the sauce, sauté the onion and garlic in the olive oil until turning they are golden. While they are cooking, mix together all the meatball ingredients, seasoning well and making sure everything is thoroughly combined. Divide the mince mixture in half, then halve again, then again, then once more. You should end up with 16 pieces. Roll each into a meatball, roughly the size of a walnut. The onion should be cooked by now, so put it to one side of the pan and add the meatballs and the spices from the sauce ingredients. Cook for 7–8 minutes until the meatballs are nicely browned all over. Now add the tomatoes and passata. Season generously, stirring all the ingredients together very gently so as not to break up the precious meatballs. Cook over a slow simmering heat for approximately 40 minutes. Ten minutes before the meatballs are cooked, pop the basmati and water in a saucepan with a tight-fitting lid and cook on a medium heat. If your timing's good, the meatballs and rice should be cooked at the same time. Adjust the seasoning of the meatballs and serve on top of the basmati, together with a dollop of yoghurt and perhaps a few Chapati (page 150).

Luke's Steak with Sautéed Onion Gravy

Feeds 4: Vegetarians may feel aggrieved when they read this, but we think that there is no real substitute for meat. Do be sensible, however, and only eat organic meat bought from a reputable farm or butcher. You will really notice the difference in flavour.

What you need:
4 **organic beef steaks**
3 cloves **garlic, crushed**
4 knobs **butter**
2 tbsp **extra virgin olive oil**
2 **onions, peeled and sliced into rings**
4 cups /1 l **Veggie Stock (page 69)**
sea salt and freshly ground black pepper

Homemade Chips (page 45)
green beans (optional)

What you do: First, marinade the steaks. Rub the meat with a pinch of salt, lots of pepper, 1 garlic clove and 1 tbsp of olive oil. Leave for half an hour while you prepare the onions, etc. Put a large frying pan on a medium heat and drizzle the pan with the rest of the olive oil. Pop the steaks on to cook. We cook our steaks for about 6 minutes per side as we like them quite well done, but you may feel more or less is better. Follow your taste buds. If you are making Homemade Chips, put them on now. When the steaks are almost cooked, dab each one with butter, add the onions and remaining garlic clove to the pan. Cook the steaks for a further minute and then take off the pan. Put the steaks on a plate and keep warm. Continue to cook the onions and garlic until soft and brown, then add the Veggie Stock, some more butter, another pinch of salt and another few twists of pepper. Put a lid over the pan to prevent all those yummy juices from escaping. Cook for a further 3–4 minutes, or until the stock has reduced by roughly half. Taste the gravy, adjust the seasoning if necessary. Pour the gravy into a serving dish. Serve at once with the Chips and perhaps some green beans. Enjoy your carnivorous feast!

'Hearthy' Beef and Thyme Stew

Feeds 4: Walking past a café one day, we saw the sign: 'Hearthy Beef Stew served all day'. Who are we to quibble? 'Hearthy' sounds even more wholesome than 'hearty', and this is surely one of the most fortifying meals – excellent on cold winters' nights as comfort food. And don't worry about the amount of garlic, each clove will be mellow and delicious by the time you eat it. There really aren't any accompaniments to Hearthy Beef Stew other than hot crusty bread for mopping up the juices.

What you need: 3 knobs **organic butter**
1 tbsp **extra virgin olive oil**
2 **onions, peeled and sliced into rings**
1 **leek, root cut off and sliced**
2 **carrots, peeled and cut into sticks**
300 g **organic beef, cut into cubes**
1 large **potato, peeled and chopped**
10 cloves **garlic, peeled and whole**
6 cups/1.5 l **Veggie Stock (page 69)**
2 tsp **dried or** 1 tbsp **fresh thyme, chopped**
sea salt and freshly ground black pepper

Farls (page146)

What you do: Put a large saucepan on a low heat and slosh in the olive oil and 2 knobs of butter. Sauté the onions and leek for 5–7 minutes. When they're soft and translucent, add the carrot and potato. Cook for a further 5 minutes. Now push the mixture to one side of the pan. Add the beef, with another knob of butter and cook until the beef has lost its meaty colour. Throw in the garlic cloves, mix all the ingredients together and cook for a further 4–5 minutes. Stir gently so all the ingredients are well coated in juices. Next, add the stock and herbs and season with lashings of pepper and salt. Bring to the bubble, turn down and leave to cook on a low heat for 45–50 minutes, until beautiful, bountiful smells are arising from the pot and you can't wait another minute. While your stew is doing its thing, make the Farls. Eat your stew hot with plenty of Farls smothered in butter if allowed. Not very sophisticated says Luke, but damn fine.

Peruvian Steak

Feeds 4: When Mum and Dad were first married, they spent 18 months in Peru, regularly travelling from the Altiplano down to the selva, or jungle, and the old rubber towns along the Amazon – Iquitos and Pucallapa – where all the local restaurants served this delicious version of steak and onions. Dished up with generous plates of piping hot patatas fritas, you can transform a small, and maybe not completely stunning, piece of meat into a funky feast in minutes.

What you need:
2 tbsp **extra virgin olive oil**
6 **onions, peeled and sliced**
3 cloves **garlic, peeled and crushed**
400 g **good organic steak cut into strips**
1 knob **organic butter**
sea salt and freshly ground black pepper

Homemade Chips (page 45)
Aioli (page 159)
Harissa (page 160)

What you do: Put a heavy-bottomed sauté/frying pan on a low to medium heat. Pour in the olive oil followed by the sliced onions (you can't have too many fried onions, so be generous). Sauté the onions until soft, gold and translucent, about 10 minutes. Then add the garlic and sauté for another minute or two. Now move the onion and garlic mixture to one side of the pan. On the other side, pop in your sliced steak pieces. Cook for 8–10 minutes, turning to cook all sides while making sure the onion and garlic mixture doesn't burn. When your steak pieces are cooked to your taste, with a wooden spoon or spatula mix all the ingredients together. Season with salt and freshly ground black pepper, top with a knob of butter and cook for a further minute or so until the butter is completely absorbed. Then onto the table with the whole pan (if it's a pretty one!) and allow everyone to help themselves. Serve with a big bowl of Homemade Chips, a bowl of Garlic Mayo and Harissa. Ay Caramba! You'll be beating them back from the table …

Chicken Meals

Not only do chickens give us chicken soup and the most wonderful white meat, but they also give us the universe's greatest packaging feat, eggs. When you are sensitive, chicken is a miracle food packed with protein and taste and yet relatively easy to digest. So much chicken is treated with water and other additives that much of the chicken available is probably actively harmful. So don't forget: always buy free-range, or even better organic, better for the choocks, better for the environment and much better for you.

Brian's Spicy Chicken Curry with Organic Brown Rice

Feeds 4: This is the perfect medicinal chicken curry! Although this may seem rather bizarre, it's an entirely reasonable suggestion. All the ingredients in chicken curry are in some way supportive to the immune system, which is especially important if you're feeling delicate. This is also a very tasty meal, one of those fabulous recipes that can be cooked on autopilot. This recipe has been designed and perfected by Brian and our many tasting sessions have paid off!

What you need:

2 tbsp **extra virgin olive oil**
2 **onions, finely chopped**
4 good-sized **chicken breasts, sliced into 1 cm strips**
2 cloves **garlic, peeled and crushed**
1 tbsp each **fresh rosemary and parsley, finely chopped**
4 tsp each **ground cumin and coriander**
2 tsp **turmeric**
2–3 tsp **cayenne pepper** *or* other chilli powder
6 cups/1.5 l **Veggie Stock (page 69)** *or* Chicken Stock
(page 76) *or* water
sea salt and freshly ground black pepper

2 cups/440 g **organic shortgrain brown rice**
4 cups/1 l **water**

Chapati (page 150)
bio-live natural yoghurt

What you do:

Place a large saucepan on a medium heat. Heat the olive oil, then add the onion and sauté for 5–6 minutes with the saucepan lid on. When the onion is soft push, it to one side and add the garlic, chicken and spices. Cook the chicken until it has lost its pink colour, say 5 minutes. Then mix everything in the saucepan together and add the herbs and spices. Season generously with pepper and a pinch of salt. Cook for 2–3 minutes more to bring out the flavour of the spices, then add the stock. Bring slowly to the boil, reduce the heat and simmer gently for 15–20 minutes. As soon as the curry is cooking independently, put the rice and water into a saucepan with a tight-fitting lid, and cook for 20 minutes on a medium heat. While the rice and curry are cooking, make the Chapati, as they'll take a few minutes to prepare and cook. The curry sauce will have reduced by half, with gorgeous smells emitting from the pot when the time to eat has arrived. So serve the curry beside, not on top of, the rice – you will want to be able to taste the plain rice too, with a dollop of yoghurt and a Chapati.

Roast Chicken with Homemade Gravy

Feeds 4-6: They say you can judge a restaurant by its roast chicken. It's definitely one of those things you think you know how to cook, but when you come to do it, it's hard to get it really scrumptious. Always try to get a really good free-range bird from a reputable farmer or butcher. Here's our simple and tasty version; original and best.

What you need:
1 tbsp **extra virgin olive oil**
1 good-sized **free-range chicken**
2 **onions, unpeeled**
4–5 **carrots, scrubbed**
1 **potato, scrubbed**
1 bulb **garlic, unpeeled and whole**
3 **streaky** *or* **back rashers of bacon**
2 knobs **organic butter** (for the gravy)
several sprigs **rosemary, bayleaf and sage**
sea salt and freshly ground black pepper
4 cups/1 l **Veggie** *or* **Chicken Stock (for the gravy)**

Baked Tatties (page 43)
green beans
Green Salad (page 61)

What you do: Preheat the oven to 230°C/450°F/gas mark 8. Remove any uncookable parts (rubber bands etc!) from the chicken. Rub the bird all over with the olive oil, season with sea salt and freshly ground black pepper, and place the choock, breast down, in a large roasting tin. Place the onions, carrot and bulb of garlic around the bird and strew the fresh herbs over the bird and veggies. Jam the scrubbed potato into the larger of the chuck's cavities, season again with salt and pepper and pop into the oven. After about 30–35 minutes, remove the chicken from the oven and carefully turn over so the breast is now facing up. Cover the breast with streaky bacon, making sure the vegetables are all cooking evenly and pop everything back into the oven. Cook for another 40–45 minutes. To check if the chicken is properly cooked through, slide a skewer or a slim knife into the thigh meat, slide out and then press down with the flat of your knife against the incision; if the juices run clear and yellow, it's cooked, if there's still a taint of pink, pop back into the oven for a further 10–15 minutes. Once you're sure the chicken is cooked, lift it carefully out of the roasting tin and onto a serving plate, along with the bulb of garlic and most of the veggies. Keep 1 onion, a few cloves of garlic, 1 carrot and the potato for the gravy. Let your chicken sit, or 'rest' – a warming oven is perfect for this, for 10–15 minutes, allowing the juices and delicious tastes to run back into the meat, while you get to grips with the gravy. With your roasting tin now on the hob on a gentle heat, first remove any scorched herbs, etc., then mash down the onion, carrot and potato with the back of a wooden spoon. Put in fresh herbs and the knobs of butter and cook for several minutes. Now add the stock. Taste, adjust seasoning and allow to cook for another few minutes – you're aiming to reduce the stock by about a quarter and the longer you can bear to leave it the more scrumptious it will be. When you're ready, put the chicken on the table with a fragrant and steaming bowl of gravy alongside. Serve with lots of Baked Tatties, green beans and a Green Salad.

Chicken Sarnies

Feeds 4: These are scrummy sandwiches, perfect for picnics and fussy families who like fast-food. Ideally these should be cooked as a family, or at least as a two-person affair, to cut down on the work involved. As always, if you've found a bread that's acceptable, use it. We love farls, they take so little effort and they are impossible to beat, both health and taste-wise. And don't fret about making the mayonnaise, it's so easy.

The Chicken

What you need:
2 tbsp **extra virgin olive oil**
4 **scallions, chopped**
4 good-sized **chicken breasts, sliced into 1 cm strips**
2 cloves **garlic, peeled and crushed**
1 tbsp **fresh rosemary and parsley, chopped**
sea salt and freshly ground black pepper

The Farls

What you need:
3 cups/330 g **white spelt** *or* **organic wheat flour**
1 tsp **bread soda**
¾ cup/200 ml **water** *or* **rice, oat, soya** *or* **cow's milk**

The Mayonnaise

What you need:
2 **free-range egg yolks**
½ cup/125 ml **extra virgin olive oil**
¼ cup/62 ml **sunflower oil**
a good squeeze **fresh lemon juice**
sea salt and freshly ground black pepper

4 handfuls **salad leaves/lettuce** *or*
Green Salad (page 61)

What you do: Put all the prepared chicken ingredients into a large frying pan on a medium heat and season well. The chicken will take about 12 minutes, with occasional stirring to prevent sticking, but if you keep an eye on it, you can let it do its own thing while you prepare the Farls and Mayo. The Farls recipe is on page 146, but here are the elements of it. Combine the flour and bread soda. Add the liquid and mix until you have a soft dough. Split the dough into 4 balls and flatten each into a round 1 cm thick. Put another pan on a medium heat and sprinkle with flour. When the flour starts to brown, place a Farl onto the pan and cook for 3–4 minutes until lightly browned. Flip over and cook on the other side for a further 3–4 minutes. Do the others the same way and keep in a warm place. Now for the Mayo: combine the two oils, then get a small bowl and put the egg yolk into it. Start by adding the first drop of oil, gently mixing it into the yolk with a small whisk. Add the second drop and mix in again, always making sure to combine the last drop of oil before adding the next. Slowly increase the amount of oil, with care, so that the mixture doesn't curdle. When the egg has absorbed all the oil, add the lemon juice, season with salt and pepper to taste and set aside. The chicken should be just cooked now, so pop it into a serving dish on the table along with the Farls, Mayo and the Green Salad. Let everyone prepare their own sandwiches at the table – slit open the warm Farls, line with lettuce, pack in the diced chicken pieces, spoon in some Mayo, season generously with sea salt and freshly ground black pepper. Scrumptious!

Spiced Chicken Wraps

A spicy, Latin America-inspired variation of Chicken Sarnies is easy. Add 2 tsp each **ground cumin, coriander and chilli** when you're cooking the chicken and use Tortillas (page 144) instead of Farls. Prepare the Wraps by taking the cooked tortilla, spreading with Mayo, then adding the cooked chicken, then the green salad. Lastly, season generously. Roll up and scoff!

Bridget Jones Chicken

Feeds 4: This is the most wonderful – and incredibly simple – dish imaginable. All the ingredients are just roughly chopped, packed into a casserole, drizzled with olive oil and popped into the oven. We called it Bridget Jones Chicken because the night we first made it was the night the film came out on video. It was 'Chop! Hurl! Grind! Drizzle!' and into the oven you go! And then we all dashed for the sofa and the video.

What you need: 4 **chicken breasts,** *or* **thighs, chopped into good-sized chunks**
5 **potatoes, scrubbed and quartered**
a few slices **parma ham** *or* **smoky bacon torn into shreds**
4 cloves **garlic, peeled and whole**
2 cloves **garlic, peeled and crushed**
2 **onions, peeled and quartered**
1 bulb **fennel, chopped into chunks**
1 handful **fresh rosemary sprigs**
juice of half a lemon
3 tbsp **extra virgin olive oil**
sea salt and freshly ground black pepper

What you do: Preheat the oven to 200°C/400°F/gas mark 6. Pack all the ingredients tightly in a good-sized casserole or ovenproof dish, giving everything a good mix to ensure all the ingredients are well coated in oil and herbs. Season generously with lashings of freshly ground black pepper and sea salt and drizzle with oil. Put on the lid or cover with foil and pop into the oven. Pot roast for 1 to 1½ hours, or until the potato chunks are soft through and through.

Chicken Provençal

Feeds 4: We adore Chicken Provençal – it's one of those dishes that can be eaten at any time of the year and on any occasion whether fancy or simple. It is so easy to make, you just pop everything in to cook and when you can't bear to wait any longer, eat! This dish can prepared ahead, as the flavour improves wonderfully. It is also gorgeous in a sandwich.

What you need: 4 tbsp **extra virgin olive oil**
2 **onions, peeled and chopped**
12 cloves **garlic, peeled and left whole**
4 **chicken fillets, cut into strips**
1 **red pepper, deseeded and cut into thin strips**
1 **yellow pepper, deseeded and cut into thin strips**
4 **very ripe tomatoes, chopped**
3–4 **sprigs rosemary**
sea salt freshly ground black pepper

1½ cups/330 g **shortgrain brown rice**

What you do: Put the olive oil into a large pan with a tight-fitting lid and place pan on a medium heat. Sauté the onion in the olive oil. After 5 minutes, add the rest of the ingredients and cook, stirring frequently, until the chicken has turned white, about 4–5 minutes. Season very generously. Put the lid onto the saucepan, and leave to cook for 25–30 minutes, stirring occasionally. While the stew cooks, put the rice on to cook with 3 cups of water on a medium heat. Both the stew and rice will be cooked at the same time. Serve together, with a chunk of bread.

Chilli Chicken Dippers

Feeds 4: They are best served with chips for the full hit.

What you need:
1 cup/110 g **white spelt** *or* **organic wheat flour**
2 tbsp **extra virgin olive oil**
1 cup/250 ml **water**
1 **free-range egg white**
2 tsp **ground coriander**
2 tsp **ground chilli**
2 tsp **ground cumin**
3 good-sized **chicken breasts, sliced into 1 cm strips**
sea salt and freshly ground black pepper

a saucepan full of good quality sunflower oil

Homemade Chips (page 45)

What you do: Warm the oil on a medium-high heat while you prepare the ingredients. Sieve the flour into a bowl, make a well in the centre, add the olive oil and water and whisk to prevent lumps. Chuck in the spices, mix again and set the batter aside. Prepare the Chips and pop in to cook as soon as the oil is ready. Cook for about 10 minutes or until golden brown. Meanwhile, prepare the chicken. Now back to the batter: whip the egg white until it forms stiff white peaks, then fold the whipped egg white into the batter. Pop the strips of chicken into the bowl of batter. The Chips should be cooked by now, so put them on a plate covered with kitchen paper and keep warm while you cook the dippers. Individually pop each dipper into your waiting deep-fat fryer. Cook for roughly 10–15 minutes or until golden brown. Serve the dippers and Chips with Mayonnaise, Zingy Tomato Salsa, natural yoghurt or any other dips you like.

Yummy Treats

If you read a 'normal' cookbook, you will be forgiven for thinking there is no such thing as a junk-free dessert; if you read most alternative cookbooks, you will be forgiven for thinking that desserts are only made from dried fruit. Rubbish! Gorgeous desserts can be made for sensitive eaters; we've tried to cover every sugar craving, from the cold, sweet and sparkly Original Lemonade to the crisp, sophisticated Twice-Baked Biscotti. We hope these inspire you. Remember that these are Green, healthy, nutritious desserts – second or third helpings are not only allowed, but absolutely essential.

Creamy Ice Lollies

Makes 4: This is a very simple recipe, but it does embody our philosophy: good food need not be complicated and Green food need not be bland. We can't stress the wonders of ice lollies too strongly, so do try.

What you need: 2 **bananas, peeled and halved widthways**
3–4 tsp **local honey**

What you do: Push a lolly stick into each half of the bananas. The honey is optional, but if you are using it, just roll each banana half in the honey. Now wrap each half individually in greaseproof paper. Pop into the freezer for 3–4 hours. Scoff straight from the freezer.

Twice-Baked Biscotti

Makes approx. 25 biscuits: Wholefood diets are not normally measured in the number of biscuits you can eat, and certainly not biscuits of the delectable high-tea standard, but these are an absolute gem. An Italian recipe, the biccies are twice baked for extra crunch. We've modified them for a more Green diet.

What you need: 1¼ cups/188 g **white spelt or organic wheat flour**
1½ tsp **bread soda**
2 **free-range eggs**
3 tbsp **local honey**
1 tsp **vanilla extract**
1 cup **whole almonds**

What you do: Preheat the oven to 180°C/350°F/gas mark 4. Mix the dry ingredients in a bowl, make a well in the centre and add the rest of the ingredients. Using your hands, mix everything together until you have a soft, pliable dough, dusting your hands with flour if it gets too sticky. Lightly oil a baking tray, shape the dough into a log about 30 cm long and 5–6 cm wide. Flatten the top of the dough with a rolling pin until it's roughly 2 cm thick, then dust with flour. Using a wetted knife, score the top of the dough at 1 cm intervals, cutting two-thirds of the way down. Bake in the oven for 12 minutes until pale golden and firm to the touch. Remove from the oven and cut fully through the markings. Arrange the pieces cut side down on the tray and pop back into the oven for a further 5 minutes. Remove from the oven and leave on a wire rack to cool – for as long as you can bear to wait.

The best thing to eat with Biscotti is *Carobella*, which is available in most good health food shops. This is a wonderful chocolatey-type spread, that is in fact made from hazelnuts – a total treat when you're off sugar and cream and additive laden 'straight' chocolate. One of the ways of staying off junk food is to eat things like Carobella – if you're too hard on yourself you won't last, and you'll start incorporating the junk back into your diet. So, be nice to yourself and buy yummy things; in the long term they're not expensive because unlike so much of 'straight' food, they're not going to make you ill.

Raspberry and Yoghurt Fool

Feeds 2: A simple and excellent combination, this gorgeous recipe can be pulled together in minutes, illustrating how a good, Green, healthy dessert does not necessarily mean carrot cake. This is also very easy to digest and good for you. You can use other berries in season, for example blackberries.

What you need: 250 g/½ a large pot **bio-live natural yoghurt**
1 cup **fresh raspberries**
2 tbsp **local honey**

What you do: Put the raspberries and honey into a bowl and mash gently, but be careful not to turn them into a total pureé. Add the yoghurt and swirl through the raspberries so that you have pink, streaky fool. Serve chilled, or at once if you can't wait, with Shortbread (page 135) if you have time to make it.

Raspberry and Yoghurt Fool (page 128): there's no fool quite like a Raspberry Fool!

Indulgence Chocolate Cake (page 138)

Twice-Baked Biscotti (page 127)

A Green Brown Bread – the staff of life (page 151)

Toast

Cheese-Butty Chilli Sarnies (page 57). You haven't lived until you've tasted these beauties.

Harissa (page 160): hot flushes all round!

Baked Nectarines

Feeds 4: This is being written in the middle of the snow, in minus temperatures in winter … Not very seasonal. However, Roast Nectarines are in fact gorgeous in the middle of winter – hot, sweet and tasty with a gooey raspberry sauce. Stylish enough for the food-for-friends thing, try serving them with natural yoghurt and Shortbread – and you really can say 'here's one I made earlier'.

What you need: 6 **nectarines, halved and stoned**
6 tbsp **local honey**
1 cup **raspberries**

What you do: Preheat the oven to 200°C/400°F/gas mark 6. Place the nectarines cut-side up on a baking tray. Drizzle each with half a tbsp of honey. Divide the raspberries evenly between each half and place in the centre. Bake in the oven for 10 minutes. Serve 3 nectarines halves per person with the gooey honey, dissolving raspberries and some Shortbread (page 135).

Original Lemonade

Makes 1 quantity lemonade stock: This makes very tasty lemonade, which is good if you care at all about your body. 'Normal' lemonade is pure sugar and junk. We've given a guide amount of honey, so if you like it sweeter just add more. It's always best to use organic, or at least unwaxed lemons when you're using the rind, as 'normal' lemons are covered in wax! Not very tasty. You can buy unwaxed/ organic lemons at most big supermarkets.

What you need: 6 cups/1.5 l **water**
4 **organic (unwaxed if organic not available) lemons**
8 tbsp **organic honey**

fizzy water

What you do: Boil the water in the saucepan. Using the thickest setting on your grater, grate the rind down to the pith of each lemon. Add the rind to the pot. Simmer gently for 5–6 minutes. While that's cooking, cut the lemons in half and juice them. Now add the honey to the pot. Stir until melted and strain the mixture into a pretty jug. Discard the rind. Add the lemon juice to the jug. Taste to check it's sweet enough and stir. You now have a lemonade base. To serve, fill a glass one third to a half full with the base and top up with fizzy water and ice.

Mango Sorbet

Feeds 4: Ice-cream for kids, sorbet for adults and heaven for those on a diet of any description.

What you need: 1 large **very ripe mango**
2 **bananas**
½ cup/125 ml **rice, oat *or* cow's milk**
honey (optional)

What you do: Using a sharp knife, take half the skin off the mango, then chop off the flesh, leaving the stone exposed. Peel off the rest of the skin and chop up the remaining flesh. Peel both bananas. Slice them up and put the mango and banana into a freezer-proof container. Pop in the freezer for 4–5 hours or overnight. Remove from the freezer and put the fruit into a blender. Slowly add the milk. Taste and add honey if it's not sweet enough for you. Put back into the container and return to the freezer for another half an hour. Remove from the freezer and serve in 4 pretty bowls.

Jammy Doughnuts

Makes approx. 10 doughnuts: These Doughnuts are inspired by Darina Allen's Balloon Recipe (from *Simply Delicious Meals in Minutes*); we've just made them more accessible. Thanks Darina. (About the jam: homemade – in your home – is best, but sugar- and rubbish-free jam will do.)

What you need: 1 cup/150 g **white spelt** or **organic wheat flour**
2 tbsp **local honey**
1 tsp **bread soda**
½ cup/125 ml **rice, oat or goat's milk**

sunflower oil for deep-frying

5 tbsp **raspberry jam**

What you do: Put the oil onto a medium-high heat. Mix the dry ingredients in a bowl. Make a well in the centre and add the honey and milk. Beat to a gloopy consistency. The oil should have been heating up for about 7 minutes now, so get a tablespoon of mixture and, using your finger, push the mixture off the end of the spoon into the hot oil, being very careful. Repeat. Cook the doughnuts for 4–5 minutes or until golden. Remove from the oil and drain on kitchen paper. Half cut each doughnut along its middle and put in 2 tsp jam per doughnut. Serve at once while still warm.

Honey Flapjacks with Lemon

Makes 10–12 biscuits: Flapjacks may sound a bit fuddy-duddy but they are a wonderful treat when you're really sensitive, as very few people have a problem with honey. They are also quite similar to 'normal' biscuits, so if you're having problems adjusting to a Green diet they are great. The only problem is not scoffing the mixture before it gets anywhere near the oven.

What you need:
4 tbsp **sunflower oil**
4 tbsp **local honey**
1 tbsp **lemon juice, freshly squeezed**
2 cups **oat flakes**
2 cups **jumbo oat flakes**

What you do: Preheat the oven to 190°C/350°F/gas mark 4. Melt the honey, oil and lemon juice in a large saucepan on medium heat, letting the mixture come to the boil. When melted, remove from the heat. Add the remaining ingredients. Stir and mix until gooey. Spread out on an oiled baking tray and pop into the oven for half an hour or until crisp and golden. Slice the flapjacks into 4 x 4 cm squares while still hot. Allow to cool, then eat at once or store in an airtight tin.

Cheat's Hot Chocolate

Feeds 2: As wrong as this may sound, it really does work. The recipe came to me after I spotted a box of carob powder in our local heath food shop and it tastes absolutely perfect. I prefer to use oat milk, but it's a matter of personal choice. As I have said, carob powder can be bought in health food shops but if you prefer, you can use pure, junk-free cocoa powder instead of the carob.

What you need: 2 cups/500 ml **oat, rice, soya, goat's *or* cow's milk**
1 heaped tsp **carob powder**
1 tbsp **local honey**

What you do: Heat your chosen milk over a medium heat for 3–4 minutes or until nearly boiling. Remove from the heat, whisk in the carob and honey until bubbly. Taste and add more honey if necessary. Serve at once.

Banana Brûlé for Brigid, with Sweet Shortbread

Feeds 2: Banana Brûlé is seriously tempting. A highly nutritious dessert, the caramelised honey is to die for and the contrast between the gooey Brûlé and the crunchy, melt-in-the-mouth Shortbread is fabulous. We find Shortbread essential to Brûlé, so we've entwined the two recipes, but you can of course just have the Brûlé without shortbread. In fact this is a children's dessert masquerading as a grown-up's treat.

Brûlé

What you need:
5 **bananas, peeled and chopped**
300 ml **organic bio-live natural yoghurt**
4 tbsp **local honey**

Shortbread

What you need:
1¼ cup/170 g **white spelt** *or* **organic wheat flour**
1 knob/50 g **organic butter**
2 tbsp **local honey**

What you do: Make the Shortbread first. Preheat the oven to 180°C/350°F/gas mark 4. Put the flour in a bowl, rub in the butter, add the honey and mix – you may need to add a drop or two of water to make the dough stick. On a floured surface roll out the dough to 1 cm thick. Cut into rounds using a normal drinking glass, re-rolling the dough until it is all used up. Pop the Shortbread onto a floured tray and into the oven for 10–15 minutes or until pale golden. While the Shortbread is cooking, make the Brûlé. Put the bananas, yoghurt and 1–2 tbsp of the honey into a pretty, flat-bottomed dish. Roughly mash together, smooth down and put into the fridge to chill while you make the Brûlé. Place a heavy-bottomed saucepan on a high heat and add the rest of the honey, which will start to bubble. Keep on the heat while stirring for 4–5 minutes until the honey is turning golden, then drizzle over the banana mixture. Return to the fridge and leave until the Shortbread is cooked. Serve together.

Live Yoghurt with Honey and Almonds

Feeds 2: Chupi first truly appreciated this simple-pick-me up dessert when, having not eaten for 36 hours due to the flu, she collapsed at the kitchen table crying 'food!' and was revived by 3 glasses of this wonderful stuff. Hope you enjoy it too. Even if you are dairy intolerant, you may well be able to tolerate organic bio-live natural yoghurt.

What you need: 250 g/½ a large pot **organic bio-live natural yoghurt**
½ cup **whole almonds, halved**
1 tbsp **local honey**

What you do: Get two pretty glasses and divide the yoghurt between them. Swirl the honey over each and add the almonds. Serve!

Carob Brownies *or* Indulgence Chocolate Cake *or* Layered Strawberry and Vanilla Cake

Makes 12 brownies: You want a multi-purpose cake recipe that actually works? You got it. We've tried numerous alternative cake recipes with dismal results. The first cake we made didn't even rise, all we got was a flat, dense pancake. However, after much practice, we produced a good, Green, cake. The first recipe makes one tray of carob brownies, but the recipe is the base for two variations. The first is for a vanilla cake layered with strawberries and cream and the other for a chocolate cake layered with chocolate and cream. For the carob powder you can use pure, junk-free cocoa powder if you want.

Carob Brownies

What you need:
4–5 tbsp **local honey**
60 g **organic butter** *or* **suitable unhydrogenated margarine**
2 **free-range eggs**
1 tsp **vanilla extract**
1¼ cups/188 g **white spelt** *or* **organic wheat flour**
2 tsp **bread soda**
3 tsp **carob powder**

1 **carob chocolate bar (if possible)**

What you do: Preheat the oven to 180°C/350°F/gas mark 4. Line a 20 cm/ 8 in square cake tin with baking parchment greased with a little oil or butter. Next, roll up your sleeves! Cream the butter and honey together in a bowl until light and fluffy, about 4 minutes – basically you're beating air into the mixture to help it rise. Now lightly beat the eggs together. Sprinkle the bread soda and carob over the creamed mixture, then fold in the flour one tablespoon at a time, alternating with a small slosh of eggs (going gently, as you don't want to beat out any of that good air). Keep adding the flour and eggs until you're finished. Pour the mix into the prepared tin, smooth down and pop into the preheated oven for 20–25 minutes. Check on the brownies after about 20 minutes. Take them out when they are very nearly fully cooked, as you want them to retain some moisture. Allow to cool, then cut into squares. If you want to impress, them with a dollop of yoghurt, some carob spread and a drizzle of honey.

Indulgence Chocolate Cake

What you need: **Brownie recipe, doubled**
6 tbsp **organic bio-live natural yoghurt**
6 tbsp **carob spread**
2 tbsp **honey**

What you do: The great thing about the Brownies recipe is that it's so versatile and can be used to make divine cakes. The quantities above will produce a cake 20 x 3–4 cm high, a lovely cake but not really enough if you want to celebrate! Simply double the quantities given above and cook the mixture in two 20 cm/8 in round cake tins. (You'll need to cook the cakes for 25–30 minutes, 5 minutes more than for the Brownies.) Once the cakes have been cooked and cooled, slice each in half horizontally so you end up with 4 layers. Spread the base with 2 tbsp yoghurt, then 2 tbsp carob, then a drizzle of honey. Put the next layer of cake on, then another 2 tbsp yoghurt, 2 tbsp carob and a drizzle of honey. Add the next layer of cake, then a final layer of yoghurt, a final layer of carob and a drizzle of honey. Finally top with the last layer of cake. If you want to go completely over the top, simply cover the whole outside of the cake with the carob spread. Perfect for birthdays, parties or indulgence.

Layered Strawberry and Vanilla Cake

What you need: Brownie recipe, doubled
6 tbsp **organic bio-live natural yoghurt**
1 medium-sized punnet **strawberries, finely sliced**
2 tbsp **honey**

What you do: If the Indulgence Chocolate Cake seems a bit too chocolatey for you, then there is an alternative. As for the Chocolate Cake, use the recipe for the Brownies and double the quantities. Leave out both the carob powder and carob bar, however, as you want this cake to be chocolate free. Prepare the cake as above. Once the cakes have been cooked and cooled, slice each in half horizontally so you end up with four layers. Spread the base with 2 tbsp yoghurt, one third of the sliced strawberries and a drizzle of honey. Layer with the next slice of cake, then repeat the yoghurt, strawberries and honey combination. Add another layer of cake, then repeat the yoghurt, strawberries and honey combination and top with the last layer of cake. A very impressive summer, birthday or party cake.

Golden Apple with Orange Crumble

Feeds 4: This is a gorgeous combination of orange crumble and sweet apple. Although Apple Crumble is rather a cliché in wholefood cooking, it's still very tasty, especially during the winter. You need to peel the apples if they're not organic as there will be a build-up of toxins in the skin. If the apples are organic, you can choose whether to peel them or not.

What you need:
3 **apples, peeled and chopped**
½ cup/125 ml **water**
juice of 1 **orange, freshly squeezed**
2 tbsp **local honey**
1 tbsp **butter**
4 tbsp **sunflower oil**
1 cup **jumbo oat flakes**
1 cup **oat flakes**
½ cup/75 g **wholegrain spelt** or **organic wheat flour**
250 g or ½ a large pot **organic bio-live natural yoghurt**

What you do: Preheat the oven to 190°C/350°F/gas mark 4. Put the apples, water and half the orange juice into a heavy-bottomed saucepan and leave to stew on a low heat while you prepare the crumble. Melt the butter, sunflower oil and honey in a saucepan. Mix the jumbo oats, oats and flour together in a bowl. Combine with the honey mixture and the remainder of the orange juice. You have your crumble. The apple should be stewed enough by now, so take it off the heat and put it into a lightly greased ovenproof dish. Cover with the crumble and pop into the oven for 40 minutes or until golden brown. While the crumble is doing its thing, lightly whip the yoghurt using a hand whisk, until it forms soft peaks. Serve the crumble with a dollop of the whipped yoghurt as an excellent homely dessert.

'Sort of' Danish Pastries

Makes approx. 14: Once while in Bath, England, on holiday, we developed a ritual of getting up before everyone else, running to the local bakery, nabbing the first freshly baked sweet danish pastries and going to sit by the river to have a pre-breakfast scoff. These, a very recent invention, are a green version and imitate the real ones well, with their sticky sweet insides.

What you need: 300 g **dates, stoned and chopped**
1 cup/250 ml **water**
2 cups/450 g **white spelt** *or* **organic wheat flour**
2 tsp **bread soda**
1 **free-range egg**
3 tbsp **local honey**
1 tbsp **organic butter** *or* **unhydrogenated margarine**
⅖ cup/100 ml **organic cow's, sheep's, oat or soya milk**

1 free-range egg white

What you do: Preheat the oven to 230°C/450°F/gas mark 8. First, stew the dates in a small saucepan on a medium heat with the water. Leave for about 7 minutes while you prepare the pastry. Combine the flour and bread soda in a bowl. Rub in the butter. Make a well in the centre and pour in the honey, eggs and milk. Mix with a blunt knife until the pastry comes together, then roll out on a floured surface to about 1 cm deep x 30 x 45 cm. The dates should be in a suitable goo by now. If not, mash with a fork until smooth. Spread the date mixture evenly over the rolled-out pastry. Now roll up the dough, as if it were a swiss roll, along the longest side, tucking the pastry in as tight as you can without tearing it. Now you should have a rather odd log, which you then slice up into 14 pieces, or whirls, about every 2–3 cm. Dust your hands and a large baking sheet with flour and gently flatten each whirl out about 1.5 cm thick. Lay on your floured baking tray and, using a pastry brush, brush each pastry with some egg white. Put into the oven for about 12–15 minutes. Remove and allow to cool before scoffing.

Excellent Breads

Of all intolerances, in our opinion, wheat and yeast really are the worst. When you can't eat bread you feel so light – whoever said bread was the staff of life wasn't joking. If you have to give up ordinary wheat – what's available everywhere – finding a good substitute that actually replicates wheat can be a nightmare. We eventually found spelt – flour grown at high altitudes and dating from Roman times, that hasn't been mauled with pesticides, etc. It's the most wonderful food and even really sensitive people can tolerate it.

By far our best bread find, however, has been Farls, the most wonderful buns/baps/rolls/naans you could get – that is without including a yeast colony or two. If you have been off bread, they are the first thing you should try. We have also included two gluten-free breads for super-sensitive people, even though we find spelt acceptable. As the French – master bakers of the universe – would say, 'Un jour sans pain c'est un jour sans soleil.'

Yummy Soda Bread

Makes 1 medium loaf: When you can't eat yeast, it seems impossible to find a decent bread; this gap, however, is happily filled by traditional Irish Soda Bread. If you don't have enough time to make your own, some of the shop soda breads are OK if you're not wheat intolerant; otherwise, try this tasty recipe.

What you need: 3 cups/450 g **wholegrain spelt** *or* **organic wheat flour**
1 cup/150 g **white spelt** *or* **organic wheat flour**
1 tsp **bread soda**
1 cup/250 ml **rice, oat, soya** *or* **buttermilk**
1 tbsp **bio-live natural yoghurt**

What you do: Preheat the oven to 230°C/450°F/gas mark 8. Put the flours and bread soda into a mixing bowl and combine. Make a well in the centre, slowly add whichever liquid you've picked and the yoghurt, mixing with a wooden spoon. You should have a soft, not too sticky, dough. Gently form the dough into a round, place on a floured baking tray, and cut 3 x 1 cm deep, parallel cuts about 3 cm apart. Pop into the oven for 35–40 minutes or until the bread sounds hollow when tapped. When cooked, remove from the oven, turn upside down on a rack and allow to cool before serving.

Olive Bread

What you need: **ingredients as for Yummy Soda Bread**
3 tbsp **extra virgin olive oil**
¼ cup **black kalamati olives, stoned and finely chopped**
½ tbsp **fresh rosemary, finely chopped**

What you do: A savoury version of Yummy Soda Bread, this is really good when you feel like something a bit more sophisticated. It is especially good with cheese. Simply add the oil, olives and rosemary to the mix and proceed as above.

Tomato and Fennel Bread

What you need: **ingredients as for Yummy Soda Bread**
3 tbsp **tomato passata**
2 tbsp **extra virgin olive oil**
½ tbsp **fennel seeds**

What you do: Another version of Yummy Soda Bread, sweet with a hint of aniseed. Add the tomato passata, olive oil and fennel seeds to the mix and proceed as above.

Doña Theresa's Corn Tortillas

Makes approx. 24: Divine Latin American food! Corn tortillas are fabulous if you're eating Green as they are suitable for everyone, including coeliac sufferers. Just fill with whatever takes your fancy, roll up and enjoy. They're also wonderful as an accompaniment to spicy dishes to scoop up excess juices. When we need Corn Tortillas, we tend to take the easy route and go straight to the experts. So we asked the people behind Sabores de Mexico, the Mexican food people, to create our tortilla recipe so you can experience Mexico in your kitchen. Now, over to Doña Theresa.

What you need: 3 cups/450 g **maize flour**
½ tsp **sea salt**
1½ cups/375 ml **tepid water**

What you do: Maize or Corn Tortillas are widely used in central and southern Mexico and have formed a pivotal part of the Mexican diet since the earliest Mixteca and Mayan peoples. Be sure to buy maize flour (verify it is GMO free), sometimes called masa harina. Avoid using polenta or maize meal for tortillas. Mix the flour, salt and water to form a ball of dough. Knead the dough until smooth, about 10 minutes. Cover it with a cloth and leave to sit for 1 hour. The dough is quite brittle, so be careful. To make the tortillas, take a small amount of maize dough and form it into a little ball in your hand. Place the ball between two pieces of plastic (use a plastic food bag cut in half, or any other suitably heavy plastic). On a floured surface, roll it out until it measures 6 cm (you can't make them any bigger, as they will disintegrate) and is quite thin, about 2–3 mm. With practice you can make them even thinner. Put a dry, heavy-bottomed pan on a high heat. Once the pan is quite hot, take the tortilla in your hand and peel off one side of the plastic. Lightly flip the tortilla on to the hot pan, peel off the other side of the plastic and allow the tortilla to cook for 30 seconds on each side or until it blisters a little. Remove to a clean tea cloth and cover as you continue with the rest. Keep in a warm place until you are ready to eat. Tortillas freeze well, so any you don't eat can be stored for later.

Flour Tortillas

As you may have noticed, Corn Tortillas tend to be rather small. If you want big ones, you have to replace the maize flour with 1 cup **wholegrain** and 2 cups **white spelt flour**. If you want very light tortillas, use 3 cups **white spelt flour**. Continue as above, but make the tortilla 20 cm wide and the same thickness as above. To cook, follow instructions above. Of course, these tortillas are not gluten free.

Farls

Makes 4: One of the biggest problems resulting from not being able to eat yeast is the lack of chewy bread baps or rolls to be had. There only ever seem to be rock hard sourdoughs or bitter, wafer-thin rye breads, neither of which is much use in sandwich making. These Farls, on the other hand, are gorgeous – even Luke, who is addicted to French bread, will happily munch a Farl. You'll never have to bemoan your breadless state again. Below we've included a few variations on our basic Farl recipe and hopefully these will inspire you to experiment.

What you need: 3 cups/450 g **white spelt** *or* **wholegrain spelt** *or* **organic wheat flour**
1 tsp **bread soda**
¾ cup/188 ml **water** *or* **rice, oat, soya** *or* **cow's milk**
1 tbsp **bio-live natural yoghurt**

What you do: Put the flour and bread soda into a mixing bowl and combine. Pour in your chosen liquid and the yoghurt, mixing with a knife (strange, I know, but it works), until you have a soft, dry dough. You can shape the Farls as you please but the traditional way is to form the dough into a ball and roll out into a circle less than 1 cm thick and slice into 4 quarters. Put a heavy-bottomed pan on a medium heat and sprinkle with flour. When the flour starts to brown, place a Farl onto the pan and cook for 5–6 minutes per side until lightly browned. Take the Farl off, sprinkle some more flour onto the pan and continue with the rest. Keep in a warm place until you're ready to eat.

Olive Bread Farls

What you need: ingredients as for Farls
3 tbsp **extra virgin olive oil**
¼ cup **black kalamati olives, stoned and finely chopped**
½ tbsp **fresh rosemary, finely chopped**

What you do: A savoury version of Farls, these are really good when you feel like something different and are especially good with cheese. Simply add the olive oil, olives and rosemary to the above. Mix and cook as above.

Naan Bread Farls

What you need: ingredients as for Farls
3 tbsp **extra virgin olive oil**
¼ cup **black kalamati olives, stoned and finely chopped**
½ tbsp **fresh rosemary, finely chopped**

What you do: To be honest these aren't any different from normal Farls, they are just shaped differently! But I so adore Naans – and my version of them – that I had to include this. When you have the ball of dough, divide it into 4 pieces. Roll each piece into an oval that's slightly bigger at one end than the other. Cook as above. Serve with Indian foods in place of Naan breads.

Cheese and Chive Scones

Makes 6 scones: The cheese and chives provide contrast and add a yummy taste to the scones. They can be whipped together in a few moments and served with a bowl of soup as a nutritious, tasty meal or eaten as a snack at any time.

What you need: 2 cups/300 g **wholegrain spelt** *or* **organic wheat flour**
1 tsp **bread soda**
1 tbsp **fresh chives, chopped**
1 lump **organic sheep's, goat's** *or* **cow's cheese**
¾ cup/188 ml **water** *or* **buttermilk**

1 tbsp **bio-live natural yoghurt** (optional)

What you do: Preheat the oven to 230°C/450°F/gas mark 8. Combine the flour and bread soda. Add the chives and cheese, then the water or buttermilk and yoghurt if using. Mix well. You should have a soft, not too sticky, dough. Divide in half, then each half into 3, so that you have 6 round balls of dough. Place on a baking tray dusted with flour and pop into the oven for 15–20 minutes or until the scones sound hollow when tapped. Allow to cool, and serve as a savoury accompaniment to soup or as a snack.

'Unwholefood' Cheese and Chive Scones

Cheese and Chive Scones are very wholesome and would pass muster in any vegan restaurant. However, sometimes one feels like a scone that's a little less weighty. For 'unwholefood' scones, replace the wholegrain spelt or organic wheat flour with an equal weight of **white spelt *or* organic wheat flour**, add another lump of **cheese** and the **yoghurt**. Cook as above.

Five Star Toasted Seed Scones

What you need: ingredients as for Cheese and Chive Scones (minus the cheese and chives)
1 tbsp **poppy seeds**
1 tbsp **sesame seeds**
1 tbsp **sunflower seeds**

What you do: If you fancy something a little different, how about seed scones? Prepare the scones as above up until just before you pop the scones into the oven, leaving out the cheese and chives. Take 2 of the uncooked scones and roll in the poppy seeds, 2 in the sesame seeds and the remaining 2 in the sunflower seeds. Dust a baking tray with flour, put one of the scones in the centre and arrange the others around it. Cook as above.

Chapati

Makes 8: These are so fabulously good. Chapati are a very flat bread, like a tortilla but Indian in origin and so perfect for scooping up the juices of any spicy meal. We serve Chapati with all Indian foods.

What you need: 2 cups/300 g **white spelt** *or* **wholegrain spelt** *or* **organic wheat flour**
⅘ cup/200 ml **water**

What you do: Mix all the ingredients together to form a softish dough. If you have the time, leave the dough to prove for half an hour. Break the dough into 8 equal pieces. Roll each piece into a ball, then flatten into a circle roughly 15 cm/6 in wide and paper thin. You may need to use more flour, as this tends to make very sticky pastry. Heat a frying pan on a medium heat and dust with flour. When the flour starts to brown, pop a Chapati on the pan and cook for 3 minutes per side or until it's puffed up. Repeat with the remaining Chapati. Keep warm until you are ready to eat. Serve with Indian foods or use as a wrap for making sandwiches.

A Green Brown Bread

Makes 1 medium loaf: This was our first loaf of cutable, toastable bread, a major feat. It's not the very Greenest of breads, as we use buttermilk, although as buttermilk contains lots of good bacteria, it isn't that bad. It's so tasty, and normal, that I'm sure you'll forgive us.

What you need: 1 cup/150 g **white spelt flour**
1 cup/150 g **wholegrain spelt flour**
15 g **bread soda**
⅓ cup/50 g **pinhead oats**
⅓ cup/50 g **oats**
⅓ cup/50 g **spelt germ** *or* **oat germ**
1 cup/250 ml **buttermilk** *or* **oat milk and bio-live natural yoghurt mixed**
1 **free-range egg**
1 tbsp **honey**

What you do: Preheat the oven to 200°C/400°F/gas mark 6. Put the two flours and bread soda in a large bowl and mix well to distribute the bread soda. Now add the pinhead oats, oats and germ. Stir again, make a well in the centre, and pour in the milk, egg and honey. Combine the mixture. It will be very wet and sticky, so stir really well, as bits can get left at the bottom of the bowl. Leave the dough to stand for 5 minutes to allow the bread soda to start bubbling. In the meantime, oil a standard bread tin with sunflower oil. Now pour (I did say it was going to be wet!) the dough into your greased tin and pop into the preheated oven. The bread will take about 45 minutes, but check after 40 minutes. The loaf is cooked when it's golden brown. Take out of the oven and allow to stand for a few minutes. To remove the loaf from the tin, hold the top of the loaf, turn upside down and wallop the base of the tin. Wrap the loaf in a teatowel and allow to cool before cutting. Store in an airtight tin for up to a week, if it lasts that long!

Rosemary Foccacia

Makes 1 medium loaf: As we have said before, when you're on a diet good breads are hard to find, so this Foccacia, which makes a beautiful olive oil flat bread, is a darling. Have it on its own or, as we eat it, with savoury goodies – 'Sun'-Dried Tomatoes (page 41), a few really tasty sheep's, goat's and cow's cheeses (for Luke!) and a Green Salad (page 61). Our lazy roast dinner or, as Mum feels it should be, just a starter before the real meal!

What you need: 1½ cups/225 g **white spelt or organic wheat flour**
½ cup/75 g **wholegrain spelt flour**
3 tbsp **olive oil**
1 cup/250 ml **buttermilk or oat milk and bio-yoghurt mixed**
1 tsp **bread soda**
½ tbsp each **fresh rosemary and thyme leaves, finely chopped**

What you do: Preheat the oven to 200°C/400°F/gas mark 6. Combine the two flours, the herbs and bread soda in a large bowl, mixing well so that the bread soda is evenly distributed. Make a well in the centre of the flour and pour in your chosen liquid and the olive oil. Using a blunt knife, mix until the dough just comes together. Now get your hands into the dough and turn once or twice. Oil a baking tray size 30 x 20 cm. Roll the dough out on a floured surface and then lay it out on the tray. Drizzle with olive oil, season with salt and pepper and pop into the oven for 15–20 minutes or until golden brown. Take out of the oven and eat at once while hot. Serve with 'Sun'-Dried Tomatoes, cheeses or other savoury titbits, or in chunks with a meal.

Dr Nancy Dunne's Gluten Free Bread

Makes 1 small loaf: Dr Dunne is a lifelong friend of Patricia and Michael Quinn, and a lifelong worker in the field of health. This is her bread for when you can't take gluten in any form.

What you need: ⅓ cup/50 g **rice flour**
⅓ cup/50 g **maize flour**
4 heaped tsp **gluten-free baking powder**
2 **free-range egg yolks**
1 cup/250 ml **organic buttermilk** *or* **soya milk**
2 tbsp **sunflower oil**
2 **free-range egg whites, beaten till stiff**

What you do: Preheat the oven to 190°C/375°F/gas mark 5. Mix the two flours and the baking powder together, stirring well, as gluten-free flours are very fine. In another bowl combine the egg yolks, milk and oil. Slowly pour into the flour mixture, beating to prevent lumps. Fold in egg whites. The consistency should be slightly firmer than pancake batter, but not stiff like cake mix. Pour into an oiled tin, lined with oiled foil or greaseproof paper. Bake in the oven for 1 hour. The bread is baked when it turns golden brown. Don't worry if you think the bread hasn't risen – this type of bread doesn't! Gluten-free bread is best served toasted. What I'd recommend, though is that you take care of yourself and get over that gluten intolerance as soon as you can.

Green Condiments

If you have any form of allergy, sauces and condiments are an extremely problematic area as they are usually highly processed and full of junk. They should make you go 'wow' when they hit you with their amazing natural flavours, but not because they contain sugar, MSG, or lashings of salt. The only solution is to make your own at home. All our sauces take only a few minutes to make, ready to be whipped together when called for. Green Condiments are also a great way to get into cooking – it's so hard to get something like Harissa wrong, you'll feel inspired to try the rest of our gorgeous recipes!

Classic Tomato Sauce

Makes approx. .5 l: Tomato sauce is one of the most versatile sauces in the world. You can use it in so many different ways – with pizza or pasta, with Baked Tatties (page 43) or Homemade Chips (page 45). This sauce is a sort of ketchup replacement, but it tastes so much better!

What you need:
2 tbsp **extra virgin olive oil**
3 cloves **garlic, peeled and crushed**
3 **scallions, cleaned and chopped**
2 **onions, peeled and chopped**
2 tins **tomatoes, chopped**
1 cup **tomato passata**
1 tbsp **fresh basil, torn**
few sprigs **rosemary, chopped**
sea salt and freshly ground black pepper

What you do: Sauté the onion, garlic and scallions in the olive oil for 8–10 minutes on a medium heat with the saucepan lid on. Stir occasionally to prevent sticking. When the onions are soft, add the tomatoes, passata and herbs. Season generously. Cook for a further 15–20 minutes until the flavours of the sauce have fully developed. You can liquidise the sauce or leave as it is, depending on what you want to use it for. Use at once or allow to cool. Store in the fridge for 3 days or freeze and reheat when required.

Fake Garlic and Herb Butter

Makes 1 quantity: Most people like garlic butter, so if you have to remove it from your diet, you can replace it with this recipe. The only real work is peeling the garlic cloves. It's much better for you than 'normal' garlic butter, whether you are dairy intolerant or not and it can be used as a dip, spread or as a sauce. It will keep for up to a week in the fridge.

What you need: 3 cloves **garlic, peeled and crushed**
3 tbsp **extra virgin olive oil**
1 knob **organic butter, preferably warm**
½ tbsp **flat-leaf parsley, finely chopped**
¼ tbsp **rosemary, finely chopped**

What you do: Combine all the ingredients in a small bowl, mixing well to ensure the butter and oil blend. These two ingredients are not going to love each other totally, so just give it a mix before you use it to ensure you get a bit of everything. Serve as a dip, spread or sauce.

Feta and Sage Relish

Makes 1 quantity: This sweet/savoury relish is good with roast potatoes, on top of toast or as a sandwich filling.

What you need:
1 tbsp **extra virgin olive oil**
1 knob **organic butter**
1 **onion, peeled and finely chopped**
2 cloves **garlic, peeled and crushed**
about 12 **fresh sage leaves, finely chopped**
2 tsp **dried** or 1 tbsp **fresh basil**
1 chunk **your favourite cheese (we use feta)**

What you do: Warm the olive oil and butter in a heavy-bottomed saucepan. Add the garlic and onion. Sauté for 5–6 minutes until the onion is soft and translucent. Add the sage, basil and cheese a minute before you serve, stirring so that the cheese melts. Serve with a roast potato, a fresh Farl or as a sandwich filling.

Zingy Tomato Salsa

Makes 1 quantity: We are addicted to the salsa from Temple Bar Food Market and this is our attempt to recreate its peppery tomato taste. Salsa is an excellent accompaniment: with a toasted Farl, some goat's cheese, atop a burger or as part of a light salad lunch. Try and make the salsa a few hours before you plan to eat it, to allow time for the flavours to develop.

What you need:
3 **scallions, finely chopped**
3 cloves **garlic, crushed**
1 tbsp **extra virgin olive oil**
7 raw **very ripe tomatoes, chopped**
1 tsp each **ground cumin, chilli and coriander**
1 tbsp each **fresh parsley and coriander, finely chopped**
sea salt and freshly ground black pepper

What you do: Mix all the ingredients together and season generously. Salsa can be stored in the fridge with a covering layer of olive oil for 3–4 days. Serve as a sauce, topping, dip or sandwich topping.

Zingier Tomato Salsa

If you want to further enliven the Salsa, add 1 **medium-hot chilli, very finely chopped**, to the above.

Mayonnaise

Makes 1 quantity: Mayonnaise from a jar is at worst full of horrendous chemicals, emulsifiers and preservatives, at best lashings of sugar vinegar. It only takes a little skill to make up your own – try this and you'll never buy another jar of your favourite brand. For health reasons, use the best free-range, or even better organic, eggs. This will keep for several days in a jar in the fridge.

What you need: 1 **free-range egg yolk**
½ cup/125 ml **extra virgin olive oil**
¼ cup/62 ml **sunflower oil**
a good squeeze **fresh lemon juice**
sea salt and freshly ground black pepper

What you do: There are several secrets to making making Mayonnaise: 1. Use a small whisk, about half the size of a normal whisk. 2. Warm the bowl you're using to make the Mayo by filling with boiling water, then emptying and drying thoroughly. 3. Try to have all your ingredients at room temperature. 4. Go slowly when adding the oil. 5. Have confidence! Start by combining the two oils, then get a small bowl, warm it, and put the egg yolk into it. Add the first drop of oil, gently mix it into the yolk. Add the second drop, mix in again, always making sure to combine the last drop of oil before adding the next. Slowly increase the amount of oil – if you are not careful, it will curdle. When the egg has absorbed all the oil, add the lemon juice and season to taste. And here's Mum's magic mayo cure: Don't panic if the Mayonnaise curdles. Take a fresh egg yolk, a new bowl and slowly add the curdled mixture to the new yoke. Use as a dip, sauce, salad dressing, in sandwiches or whatever you want.

Aioli
Aioli is garlic mayonnaise, absolutely gorgeous and better than ordinary Mayo for that extra zing. Just add 1 clove garlic, **peeled and crushed**, to the egg before you start adding the oil.

Yoghurt Herb Mayonnaise
This is a creamier Mayonnaise that can be used as normal Mayo, but is better suited to people who like a mild Mayonnaise. Simply add 4 tbsp **organic bio-live natural yoghurt**, 1 tbsp **fresh chives, parsley, rosemary or mint or a mix of the four, finely chopped**, once the Mayo is made, either the Mayonnaise or Aioli recipes.

Harissa (Chilli Relish)

Makes 1 jar: When you're eating Green, suitable sauces are one of the hardest foods to locate. We use Harissa to pep up many different foods, such as burgers (veggie or not) and sandwiches. Just be careful not to add too much. Harissa will keep for days in the fridge, as long as you renew the layer of olive oil.

What you need: 9 medium-hot red chillies, deseeded and roughly chopped
1 tomato, chopped
4 cloves garlic, peeled and chopped
1 tsp each ground cumin and coriander
1 tbsp flat-leaf parsley, chopped
3 tbsp extra virgin olive oil
sea salt and freshly ground black pepper

What you do: Whizz all the ingredients to a smoothish consistency in a blender. Season generously. Store in a screw-top jar with a sealing layer of olive oil.

Green Basil Pesto

Makes 1 quantity: Pesto is so trendy, but also very healthy, as long as you make it at home. The shop-bought gunk isn't worth eating. Roasting the pine nuts is optional – they taste better, but if you're very rushed then they are fine unroasted. Pesto is mulit-functional, and you can use it in association with breads and pastas for the best results.

What you need:
1 cup **very fresh pine nuts**
3 tbsp **extra virgin olive oil**
1 squeeze **fresh lemon juice**
1–2 cloves **garlic, peeled and crushed**
2–4 handfuls **fresh basil, finely chopped**

What you do: Preheat the oven to 230°C/450°F/gas mark 8. Lay the pine nuts out on a baking sheet and pop into the oven for 10–15 minutes or until the nuts are golden brown. If using a pestle and mortar, chop up the basil then crush all the ingredients in your mortar. If using a blender, whizz all the ingredients. With a pestle and mortar you will get a rougher, chunkier Pesto. Serve as a dip or sandwich filing, with organic pasta or thinly spread across a hot piece of toast. Provided you keep a thin layer of olive oil over the pesto – renewed every time you use it – it will keep for a week or two in the fridge.

The Kitchen

When you begin the change to Green eating you will need to review both the food you have in your home and the food you buy. You may, as we have done, change your whole outlook on food and eating, or you will perhaps just want to incorporate some new things into your diet. Either way, your cupboards are where to start.

First, look through your cupboards and fridge. Examine the food you eat, read the labels and prepare to be shocked, bemused and annoyed. Now chuck out any suspicious foods and replace them with proper food. The most important thing when out shopping is to read the labels on everything. We know that a lot of people are pressed for time, but you only need do it once: look through the foods you have at home, examining the labels of the things you consider as staples. No doubt at least one of them will take you by surprise – do you know what E621 is? And why it's necessary in your Italian-style, 'health conscious' pizza? Then every time you shop, read the labels of things that you buy occasionally.

Another important thing we have learnt in our food forays is that when you have to give something up, you should replace it. We no longer use non-organic wheat flour, or any products containing non-organic wheat flour, yet we still have breads, biscuits and pizzas, because we found a replacement flour. Spelt flour is an ancient version of wheat that seems to be digestively perfectly acceptable for people who are wheat intolerant. It even tastes better.

The Golden Rules

These are the most important qualities a food can possess:

Organic This is no longer a fad – organic farming is here to stay. It heralds a return to traditional farming methods, which are cruelty, artificial, chemical and GM-free.

Locally produced Such products will be in harmony with your body. Un-forced food is more healthy and you are also supporting your local community.

In season Out of season = tonnes of chemicals to produce. If you eat seasonally, you get that lovely 'Ooh! It's courgette' (or other foodstuff)-time buzz!

Minimal amount of processing Processing reduces the nutritional content of foods and such food is usually full of junk.

Brand spankingly fresh Fresh food has a higher nutritional content, and of course food just tastes so much better when it's fresh.

Junk-free This may seem obvious, but when you're out shopping, you can sometimes to forget to check if a food is acceptable.

The Storecupboard

Out

All commercial, non-organic wheat flours
All yeast
All sugary cereals
All non-organic wheat pasta and noodles
All artificial flavourings and table salt
All refined sugar and artificial sweeteners
All junk snacks, e.g. commercial crisps
Vegetable and nondescript cooking oil
Stock cubes and other flavour enhancers
All ready made sauces and condiments
All refined rice, e.g. boil-in-the-bag
Instant coffees and teas
All instant food stuffs and ready-made meals

In

Organic spelt or organic wheat flours, both wholegrain and white
Bread soda and wheat-free baking powder
Homemade muesli and granola, junk-free cereals
Organic spelt, wheat or buckwheat pasta, rice noodles and millet
A grinder of black pepper and of sea salt
Local organic honey
Organic crisps, sweets, Bombay mix, dates, almonds, popcorn, peanuts
Extra virgin olive oil and sunflower oil (organic)
A pot of fresh stock and yeast-free bouillon powder
Homemade pesto, Harissa and salsa
Organic shortgrain brown rice and white basmati
Dandelion coffee and herbal teas, e.g. camomile
Fine ingredients to prepare your own meals: Organic tinned tomatoes, chickpeas, kidney beans, mixed beans, tuna, red and green lentils, oats

The Fridge

Out

All processed cheeses
Non-organic dairy butter and 'normal' margarine
All non-organic dairy milks, including low fat
All artificially flavoured yoghurts
All non free-range eggs
All processed suspect sauces and relishes, e.g. mayonnaise, ketchup and soy sauce
All sugary drinks
All junk convenience foodstuffs
All non-organic meat

In

A selection organic cheeses, including cheddar and feta
Organic dairy butter
A selection of alternative milks: organic cow's, sheep's, rice, oat or soya
Organic dairy, bio-live natural and naturally flavoured yoghurts
Organic, if possible, free-range eggs
Ingredients for mayonnaise, salsa, harissa and dressing
Fresh fruit juices, sugar-free fizzy drinks and smoothies
Fresh ingredients
Organic meat: minced beef, chicken fillets, bacon
Organic fruit and veg: onions, garlic, tomatoes, scallions, potatoes, avocado and seasonal green veg, e.g. courgettes in late summer, cabbage in winter, bananas, lemons and apples

Everything you buy will not meet these criteria all the time, but this is what we should all aspire to. Don't feel overwhelmed if it seems impossible – everyone starts somewhere, and hopefully you'll become so passionate about food and eating you'll want to find the best. Good luck!

The Garden

This section is dedicated to Michael 'Mr Green Fingers' Quinn. Why the garden? If you try to buy fresh herbs in a supermarket, you will be met by rows of tiny plastic boxes containing three sprigs of rosemary or six leaves of basil at an exorbitant price. Look at your garden, or your windowsill – surely there's a spot somewhere for a rosemary bush, a few pots of basil or some chives? Go to your local garden centre and buy one rosemary plant – pop it into your garden, or into a pretty pot on your windowsill, and watch it thrive. Use sprigs of rosemary when you cook, it is so easy, so cheap and so delicious. Now that you are hooked, read our list of 'must have' herbs and go get them.

Basil Wonderful in all dishes that contain tomatoes or anything Mediterranean, basil regulates the adrenal system, helping our bodies to relax and cope with stress. Basil grows only in the summer, must be grown in pots and needs to be watched as greenfly love it. That said, it is so gorgeous you can forgive these minor faults.

Bay A truly magnificent herb, or should that be tree – we have a bay bush which is now 12 feet high! Don't let that put you off, though. Bay leaves are an essential ingredient in stock and for all roasting dishes.

Chives Also known as cheat's onions, chives are perfect when you want the onion hit without the work. They are antibacterial and share other health giving characteristics with the other members of their family – onions, scallions and garlic. Very easy to grow, chives take up a minimum of space and produce pretty purple flowers too.

Mint Excellent for enlivening salad dishes, mint cleanses the system wonderfully if you're feeling a bit stodgy. Simple to grow, mint will happily occupy an entire bed to itself. You can contain it by planting it in a large colander.

Parsley Another cleanser, parsley is also very high in vitamin C, perfect if you have the flu. Parsley is an 'easy' herb, not so strong as to put people off, so it can be safely put into nearly all dishes as a natural flavour enhancer. Again, it is easy enough to grow, but best grown in pots.

Rosemary Without a doubt my favourite herb. Rosemary and basil have a natural affinity and are gorgeous together. Rosemary works in traditional (potato cakes), Mediterranean (Cianfotta), and our food (fried rice). It is also easy to grow, provided you find a nice dry, free-draining spot.

Sage Quite a robust flavour, sage is best used where you can really taste it, such as in Feta and Sage Relish, or else as part of a bouquet of herbs in a stew or stock. Sage is a wonderful healer, perfect with lots of honey for sore throats, 'flu or colds. Sage likes the same growing conditions as rosemary, a dry, hot undisturbed spot.

Thyme Where would any stew be without thyme? Thyme is perfect with rosemary and sage, popped in beside any dish to be roasted. Its warm flavour is wonderfully comforting. Like sage, thyme is a great healer, though it is better suited to the lungs. Thyme will happily grow beside sage and rosemary.

Food Resources

Resources for good food are crucial. When you change your eating habits, you also need to change where you shop and what you buy. In The Kitchen we dealt with what you buy, here we'll try help you with where to shop. Remember, though, always to read the label – only you know what you can and can't eat. Don't be fooled if something says 'healthy', and just because a packet says sugar/dairy/wheat/yeast-free, it doesn't mean it's not packed with other artificial rubbish. As Dr Jane Plant, the British scientist and author of *Your Life in Your Hands*, says, never go out without your glasses and read **all** labels.

Local Shops

By local shops we mean the greengrocer, the butcher and the deli, each a valuable resource. Mostly ignored in favour of giant supermarkets, local shops are a great ally. Their produce is often less likely to be processed than supermarkets' and they know where the food they stock comes from. Small shops, unlike the supermarkets, don't have the resources to buy food from halfway across the globe and freeze it for months on end, so use this to your advantage. Local food shops tend to be very keen on their food so ask what's best and what's organic and local. Create a demand!

Health food Shops

If you've never been into your local health food shop, start today. It may appear intimidating, but persevere and you'll find most staff in such shops are ready and willing to help. They are also good for information on local organic farms with box schemes, for example, and they're always happy to source anything you need. In such stores, you'll find all store-cupboard staples e.g. spelt flour, local organic food and Green packet foods, e.g. falafel mix.

Farmers' Markets

These are the fastest growing new food outlets at the moment. Farmers' markets are a gift to the Green eater: tasty, organic, just harvested-this-morning, not-too-expensive food straight from the producer. Could you ask for anything better? Look around your locality, there's bound to be some sort of market near you. We go to Temple Bar Food Market in Dublin, the Laragh farmers' market in Glendalough and the local Country Market (run by the Irish Countrywomen's Association), in Blessington. At posher markets you'll find tasty treats, e.g. good olive oil, and other specialities. Farmers' markets will supply you with local veg, fruit, bread and meat
Country markets are where you will find free-range eggs, local honey, soda breads, seasonal fruit and veg.

Supermarkets

You may be surprised by what you can now find in your supermarket. Most stock a good range of Green foods and are bowing to the inevitable Green food revolution! They are good for cheap organic store-cupboard staples, e.g. tinned tomatoes and organic dairy produce.

Tools of the Trade

To get cooking in both style and comfort, these are the items you will need.

Knives

2 or 3 good chef's knives (French Sabbatier are best). 1 medium blade (12 cm), and 1 small blade (8 cm) for peeling and paring. Invest in the best you can, as you'll be using them all the time.

1 good breadknife (21 cm). Get one with really good teeth and a strong, comfortable handle.

Chopping Boards

2 or 3 good solid wooden boards for chopping and preparing.

Gadgets and Gizmos

Knife sharpener We use the flat kind that sits on the table.

Garlic press Try and get the metal kind – the plastic ones tend to snap under pressure.

Can opener You need a good strong one.

Peeler The metal blade kind with a bound wooden handle; the plastic ones break and all metal ones hurt your hands.

Kitchen scissors A good strong scissors that is kept just for use in the kitchen.

Box grater A wonderful gizmo, essential for grating and zesting jobs.

Potato masher The all-metal kind are good.

Pepper mill Totally essential. Salt mills are good too, but not essential.

Citrus juice squeezer Rigid plastic will do, but you can sometimes find beautiful old glass ones.

Measuring jug We have a big and a small one. Make sure they have metric and imperial measures. Glass, or pyrex, are best.

Weighing Scales An add and weigh scales is most convenient.

Whisk We have 1 large and 1 medium.

Sieve The old-fashioned metal kind are best.

Rolling pins We have two wooden ones, large and small.

Spoons

2 or 3 wooden spoons and 2 wooden spatulas Absolutely essential, we have lots of wooden spoons.
Metal ladle (for soups, stews, etc.)
Fish slice

Pots and Pans

1 large heavy-bottomed cast iron frying/sauté pan
2 medium size non-stick frying/sauté pans
2 or 3 good quality stainless steel pans (large/medium/small)
2 or 3 cast iron enamelled pans. Le Creuset are best, if expensive, but once you have one you'll have it for life.
1 large roasting tin The deep enamelled tins are best.
1 loose-bottomed cake tin (16–18 cm)
1 loose-bottomed pizza/quiche tin (30 cm)
1 wire rack For cooling and for cooking.

Electrical Gear

1 hand-held electric whizzer/blender This is all you need. You can dispose of your enormous 'processor'. Once you've got the hang of the hand-held blender, you'll never take that other complicated, breakable, difficult-to-wash gadget out of the cupboard *ever* again.

Index